A Beginner's Guide
to the Books of the Bible

Augsburg Beginner's Guides introduce readers to key subjects in the past and present of the Christian tradition. Beginner's Guides strive to be readable and yet reliable, simply written but not simplistic in their approach. Each book in the series includes the information that is needed for an overview of the subject and as a solid foundation for further study.

A Beginner's Guide to Reading the Bible
   by Craig R. Koester

A Beginner's Guide to the Books of the Bible
   by Diane L. Jacobson and Robert Kysar

A Beginner's Guide to Studying the Bible
   by Rolf E. Aaseng

A Beginner's Guide to

THE
BOOKS
OF THE
BIBLE

Diane L. Jacobson
and
Robert Kysar

Augsburg ▪ Minneapolis

A BEGINNER'S GUIDE TO THE BOOKS OF THE BIBLE

Scripture quotations unless otherwise noted are from the New Revised Standard Version of the Bible, copyright © 1989 by the Division of Christian Education of the National Council of the Churches of Christ in the United States of America.

Cover design and illustration: Catherine Reishus McLaughlin

Library of Congress Cataloging-in-Publication Data

Jacobson, Diane L., 1948–
    A beginner's guide to the books of the Bible / Diane L. Jacobson
and Robert Kysar.
      p. cm.
   ISBN 0-8066-2572-4 (alk. paper)
   1. Bible—Introductions. I. Kysar, Robert. II. Title.
III. Title: Books of the Bible.
BS475.2.J334 1991
220.6'1—dc20

91-36711
CIP

The paper used in this publication meets the minimum requirements of American National Standard for Information Sciences—Permanence of Paper for Printed Library Materials, ANSI Z329.48-1984. ∞™

Manufactured in the U.S.A.   AF 9-2572

00   99   98   97   96   4   5   6   7   8   9   10   11   12   13

Contents

Publisher's Preface 7

Authors' Preface 9

PART 1: THE OLD TESTAMENT 11

The Pentateuch ...12   Genesis 14
                             Exodus 16
                             Leviticus 18
                             Numbers 20
                             Deuteronomy 21

The Historical   Joshua 24
Books 23   Judges 26
                             Ruth 27
                             1 and 2 Samuel 28
                             1 and 2 Kings 31
                             1 and 2 Chronicles 34
                             Ezra and Nehemiah 36
                             Esther 38

The Psalms   Job 41
and Wisdom   Psalms 42
Literature 40   Proverbs 44
                             Ecclesiastes 46
                             Song of Solomon 47

The Prophets 48   Isaiah 51
                             Jeremiah 53
                             Lamentations 56
                             Ezekiel 57
                             Daniel 59

Hosea 61
Joel 62
Amos 63
Obadiah 65
Jonah 65
Micah 67
Nahum 68
Habakkuk 69
Zephaniah 71
Haggai 72
Zechariah 73
Malachi 75

PART 2: THE NEW TESTAMENT 77

The Gospels 79
Matthew 80
Mark 82
Luke 84
John 86

**Historical
Narrative 88**
Acts 88

**The Letters
of Paul 91**
Romans 92
1 Corinthians 94
2 Corinthians 96
Galatians 98
Ephesians 99
Philippians 101
Colossians 103
1 Thessalonians 104
2 Thessalonians 105

**The Pastoral
Letters 107**
1 Timothy 108
2 Timothy 109
Titus 109
Philemon 110

**Hebrews and
the "Catholic
Letters" 111**
Hebrews 112
James 115
1 Peter 116
2 Peter 118
1 John 119
2 John 120
3 John 121
Jude 122

Apocalyptic 123
Revelation 123

6

Publisher's Preface

The many differences that exist among the sixty-six books of the Bible can be confusing to modern readers. This book presents basic information about each of the books of the Old and the New Testaments in an easy-to-follow format.

A Beginner's Guide to the Books of the Bible not only gives concise introductions to each of the books, but also calls attention to a number of passages of great beauty or particular quality. The authors highlight messages of comfort, warning, lament, or rejoicing that have been remembered and cherished by God's people through the centuries—messages that still speak to us today.

Individuals will find this book to be a valuable resource for their personal Bible reading or study, and groups or classes will appreciate its summaries as they begin a Bible study or discussion.

Authors' Preface

Reading the Bible can be one of the central joys of life and one of the principal means of encountering God. People can learn from Scripture—be instructed, inspired, and drawn into the world that is offered there. But we who have written this guide, ourselves longtime teachers and passionate readers of the Bible, know that instruction and inspiration are difficult without some basic knowledge of the sixty-six books which make up this marvelous text.

We have written this *Beginner's Guide to the Books of the Bible* for new readers of the Bible who want a preview before they begin, for those who want a quick overview of a biblical book to put a passage or quotation in context, and for those already familiar with the Bible who wish to refresh their memories about the content, background, and central messages of an individual book.

The format of this guide is straightforward. General introductions to the Old and New Testaments as well as introductions to the various sections of the Bible (for example, Pentateuch, Prophets, Gospels, Letters of Paul) precede the discussions of the individual books. Information is given about the dates, authors, historical backgrounds, purposes, settings, and literary types.

Additionally the contents of each book are briefly summarized, and the major emphases are highlighted in the sections labeled "distinctive features" and "central themes."

The information in this guide is by design concise and direct. While we have drawn upon the most up-to-date scholarship available to us and incorporated the insights of numerous colleagues, we have avoided the use of footnotes and technical language. A good deal of information is packed into a few pages, and hopefully many readers will wish more detailed background and interpretive information to follow up this guide. A reader might look at a one-volume commentary like *Harper's Bible Commentary* or at commentaries on individual books such as those found in *Augsburg's New Testament Commentaries* or John Knox's *Interpretation* series. We hope the short introductions offered here are helpful, and we wish you many fruitful and fulfilling hours reading and studying the Scriptures.

Diane L. Jacobson
Robert Kysar

Part 1

The Old Testament

The Old Testament, which makes up the first section of the Christian Bible, contains thirty-nine books that form a glorious, sometimes complicated, collection of sacred texts. These books tell of the dynamic relationship between God—Creator and Redeemer, whose way is both merciful and just, frightening yet compassionate—and the people Israel—who struggle to know and obey God, who are sinful and fallen on the one hand, visionary and uncompromisingly faithful on the other. The Old Testament expands this relationship between God and Israel to include reflections on the broader relationship between God and all people, between God and all the world. As such, the Old Testament forms a crucial part of Christian Scripture—a part that reveals the nature of God's encounter with humanity and the world. The Old Testament is challenging and inviting, but not always easy to follow. This introduction attempts to help in the process.

The books of the Old Testament present multiple perspectives through different types of literature. Included, for example, are stories and psalms, laws and proverbs, history and legend, prophetic proclamations and love songs. The history that stands behind these books ranges over two millennia before the birth of Christ—from the days of the patriarchs and matriarchs (2000–

1750 B.C.) to the time of the Exodus from Egypt (1350–1250); from the days of the Judges (1200–1000) to the united kingdom of David and Solomon (1000–922); from the divided kingdoms (922) to the fall of the Northern Kingdom of Israel to Assyria (722–721) and the fall of the Southern Kingdom of Judah to Babylon (587–586); from the end of the exile in Babylon (538) to the days of Ezra and Nehemiah and the rebuilding of the temple in Jerusalem (538–515) in the days of Persian rule (538–333) and, finally, Hellenistic domination (333–164). The action takes place mainly in the tiny land of Israel (6,000 square miles), set between the vast empires of Egypt (ruled by numerous dynasties) and Mesopotamia (variously ruled by Assyria, Babylon, and Persia).

The Protestant arrangement of the books of the Old Testament, which varies slightly from the order found in Jewish and Roman Catholic traditions, divides the thirty-nine books into four parts: The first five books are identified as the Pentateuch. The next twelve books are often labeled the historical books, though in the Jewish tradition these are called "The Former Prophets." The historical books continue the story begun in the Pentateuch. The third section contains the writings, which include wisdom literature and psalms. Finally come the prophetic books, which include the three major prophets plus Lamentations and Daniel as well as the twelve minor prophets. (The Roman Catholics also include some additional books called the Apocrypha.) Despite the complications that regularly arise, reading these books can be an exciting and challenging adventure.

The Pentateuch

The Pentateuch, or "five books," includes Genesis, Exodus, Leviticus, Numbers, and Deuteronomy. In Jewish tradition these books are called Torah, or "teaching," which combines both the story (Haggadah) and the law (Halachah). The message of the Pentateuch evolves from the creative tension between story, which inspires and forms the basis of community identity, and law, which directs and orders life within the community.

Authorship and Date. Discussions about the authorship of the Pentateuch are complicated, often confusing, and remain speculative. Tradition has identified Moses as the author because of his central role as both lawgiver and leader of the people of Israel. Scholars down through the ages, particularly in modern times, have come to understand the Pentateuch and much of the rest of Scripture as the work of the larger community. Traditions from the community were passed down in both oral and written form throughout the long period of Israel's history. At various stages and places, these traditions were composed and compiled into works which eventually were combined into the five books we now have, probably shortly after the Babylonian exile.

Contemporary scholars have identified four key compilers or composers of the Pentateuch in an attempt to untangle the web of Pentateuch traditions. The four "authors" and their intertwined documents are identified using the letters J, E, D, and P. J, who prefers to use the name of Yahweh (*J*ahweh in German) for God, signifies the form of the tradition that comes from *J*udah during the reign of David (1000–950). This work centers on the centrality and dependability of God's promises. E, who refers to God as *E*lohim, represents the tradition that comes from the Northern Kingdom, sometimes called *E*phraim. This tradition, written after the division of the kingdom but before the fall of the North, places emphasis on God's word and the need for obedience. D, or the *D*euteronomist, is mainly responsible for the book of Deuteronomy. This work represents Northern traditions reworked from a Southern perspective. The written work combines material from the time of King Josiah (640–609), as well as from times just prior to and following the Babylonian exile. This writer and his school of followers were responsible as well for the editing of the history books that follow. (See the sections "Deuteronomy" and "The Historical Books.") P represents the *P*riestly traditions of Jerusalem compiled both before and during the exile. This tradition reflects concern for law and worship, obedience to God's pronouncements, and the proper ordering of the tradition.

Theoretically, these works had a separate identity and perhaps even a life apart from each other, like the four Gospels. The Pentateuch as we now have it represents a compilation of these traditions, leaving in conflicts and discrepancies, even some duplicated accounts. While a great deal of energy has been and can be invested in distinguishing these four authors, their existence and dates remain speculative, and their importance should not be overestimated.

Issues of authorship and date should never stand in the way of reading the Pentateuch as a whole with its own integrity and purpose. The movement of the text—from the creation of the world to the birth of the nation of Israel, to her redemption from slavery to her encampment on the border of the promised land— provides for us a model for understanding the nature of God's expectations and promises. Moreover, as will become evident, each of the five books of the Pentateuch contributes its own themes.

GENESIS

Historical Background. The book of Genesis, except for the first eleven chapters, deals with the world of Israel's earliest ancestors. The action of the book moves back and forth between Mesopotamia, the land of origins and later of captivity, and Canaan, the land of the promise, and rests finally in Egypt, the land of subsequent enslavement. Genesis reflects some of the history and traditions of the Middle Bronze Age (2100–1550) in which these forebears lived, particularly the strong clan identity and the mixture of peoples in the land. However, Genesis also reflects some of the underlying concerns from the times of the writers, particularly J and P. Despite the large backdrop of the purpose of creation and movement of all history, Genesis remains preeminently a family story about relationships between spouses, between parents and children, and between brothers and sisters. All of them struggle and live under the care, direction, and watchful eye of God.

Contents. The book of Genesis, or "beginning," can be divided into four sections: (1) Genesis 1–11 deals with the cosmic beginning of the earth and of history. These chapters include accounts of the creation, Adam and Eve, Cain and Abel, Noah and the flood, and the tower of Babel. (2) Genesis 12—25:18, the Abraham cycle, contains stories about Abraham, his wife Sarah, and their son Isaac, as well as stories about the slave girl, Hagar, and Ishmael, her son by Abraham. Key events center on God's calling of Abraham, his covenants with God, and the near sacrifice of Isaac. (3) Genesis 25:19—36:43, the Jacob cycle, can itself be divided into three parts, all marked by conflict and struggle. The initial stories deal with Jacob and his brother, Esau, and center on their struggles, which begin in the womb of their mother, Rebekah, and continue through fights over porridge, birthright, and blessing. The middle portion deals with Jacob's battles with his uncle Laban. Laban's daughters, Rachel and Leah, in turn struggle over Jacob's affections and the birth of children. In the midst of these struggles, eleven of the twelve sons are born who are destined to become the fathers of the tribes of Israel (Dinah, a daughter, is also born at this time whereas Benjamin, the twelfth son, is born later at Rachel's death). The final chapters bring Jacob back to Canaan to encounter once again his brother Esau. Between each of these sections, Jacob encounters divine forces, first at Bethel where he dreams of angels ascending and descending from heaven, and next at the Jabbok where he wrestles a mysterious man and encounters God face to face. (4) Genesis 37–50 presents the story of Jacob's favorite son, Joseph, whose own struggles with his brothers bring him to Egypt where he eventually rises to a position of authority in Pharaoh's court.

Distinctive Features. Genesis 1–11 sets the tone for the rest of the book by telling primeval stories that proclaim the basic relationship between God, the gracious Creator, and the world

God creates. These chapters mirror human character through pictures, on the one hand, of the joy of right relationships and, on the other, of sins against God and each other. Genesis reports two covenants that underline God's promises: the cosmic covenant made with Noah and the more particular covenant with Abraham. The genealogies provide a sense of order to the whole book, proclaiming that God's intention for the world is through Abraham and his descendants, and showing how those descendants expand from two individuals to a large extended family. Finally, even the stories that are not central to the overall movement of Genesis often serve a purpose by stressing God's relationship to those outsiders or outcasts such as Hagar and Ishmael who are not chosen, yet who remain objects of God's care.

Central Themes. Five themes are worthy of note: (1) The theme of blessing is evident in Genesis 1 when God blesses all he has made. Later, God tells Abraham his descendants shall be a source of blessing for all the families of the earth (12:1-3). (2) The theme of election (being chosen) concerns God's special purpose for Israel. The continual ascendancy of the younger sons over the elder shows that election comes from God. (3) With Abraham begins the theme of divine promises of land and descendants. Despite numerous obstacles such as old age and barrenness, disobedience and disbelief, famine and the indigenous population of Canaan, God's promise remains steadfast. (4) The theme of human strife and deception appears throughout Genesis. This theme creates tension between deception and blessing, between struggle and election. (5) Finally, the theme of the overall providence of God comes to the fore in the story of Joseph. Together these themes help Christians forge community identity and help them read Genesis as a reflection of our foundational relationship with God.

EXODUS

Historical Background. The most probable historical setting for Exodus is Egypt's new kingdom (1550–1070 B.C.). As in

16

Genesis, concerns and traditions from the times are blended with and reinterpreted by traditions of J, E, and P (see pp. 13-14). The laws in Exodus are among the oldest in the Pentateuch; the oldest songs are the songs of Miriam and Moses in Exodus 15.

Contents.   The action of Exodus (which means "a going out" or "exiting") begins in Egypt. The descendants of Jacob had become slaves, subject to hard labor. Pharaoh tried to kill all the male babies of Israel, but Moses was saved by two midwives, his mother, sister, and Pharaoh's own daughter. After killing an Egyptian, Moses fled to the land of Midian where he received a call from God out of a burning bush. Moses was called to set his people free from Pharaoh's slavery and bring them to the mountain in the wilderness to worship the LORD. Together with his brother Aaron, Moses returned to Egypt and demanded the release of his people. When Pharaoh refused, God sent ten plagues, the last being the death of firstborn Egyptians. Moses led his people out of Egypt to the Red Sea. There the LORD parted the waters so that the Israelites passed over on dry land whereas Pharaoh and his troops drowned. In response to this divine act of redemption, the people sang a victory song (chap. 15). After some preliminary wandering in the desert, Moses led the people to Mount Sinai where the LORD revealed the Ten Commandments and the covenant code (chaps. 20–23) as well as laws dealing with worship (chaps. 24–31). When the people became impatient waiting for Moses to return from the mountain, they built a golden calf and worshiped it. When Moses returned, he smashed the two tablets of the law. Moses later received the law again and delivered it to the people, after which service in the tabernacle began.

Distinctive Features.   Exodus centers around two events: first, the delivery from slavery in Egypt, particularly as symbolized by the crossing of the Red Sea (chaps. 14–15), and second, the giving of the law at Sinai (chaps. 19–20), which constitutes the third covenant (the first covenant was with Noah and the second with Abraham). Also, God's name, Yahweh, usually translated "LORD," is revealed (3:13-15). In the midst of this story of salvation are found explicit directions about the festival of Passover (chap. 12), making Exodus a book that combines event, celebration, and proclamation. The laws fall into two overlapping categories: the Ten Commandments and other laws that order the society, and laws dealing with cultic matters such as the ark, tabernacle, altar, vestments, and priestly orders. The key human figure is Moses, deliverer and lawgiver, whose varied character becomes for us a study of a divinely chosen leader—imperfect and sinful, yet in constant relationship with God.

Central Themes. In Exodus the themes begun in Genesis, particularly those of election and promise, continue. Even under oppression, Israel is transformed from a family to a people, "a priestly kingdom and a holy nation" (19:6). As the primary story of redemption in the Old Testament, Exodus also contributes important themes to a Christian understanding of redemption. Redemption is communal and concerns not only spiritual but physical oppression and tyranny. Freedom *from* slavery and oppression also includes freedom *to* serve the LORD. In the great battle of Exodus, the LORD is revealed as a God of salvation and power who delivers his people from Pharaoh, a mere mortal and tyrant. Obedience to the law is portrayed within the context of covenant as the desired response to this divine deliverance.

LEVITICUS

Authorship, Date, and Purpose. Leviticus, a book of laws given by God to Israel, was compiled by the priestly writer (P) during the period of the Babylonian exile (587–538 B.C.). The priestly collector uses the setting of wilderness wanderings to show that community life under God's care is possible even outside of the promised land.

Contents. Leviticus can be divided into six, twelve, or even thirty-six parts. The six-part division is as follows: (1) laws about sacrifice (chaps. 1–7); (2) a narrative section dealing with priestly consecration and sins (chaps. 8–10); (3) laws that distinguish clean from unclean (chaps. 11–15); (4) a narrative about the day of atonement (chap. 16); (5) laws, known as the "holiness code," by which Israel orders her life as a holy people (chaps. 17–26); and (6) laws concerning vows and tithes (chap. 27). Some of the matters the levitical laws deal with are: varieties of sacrifice and offerings; priestly ordinations; dietary regulations; defilement and cleansing; festivals; proper sexual relations; ethical concerns and a life of holiness; concern for neighbor, community, and stranger; holy items and seasons; and Sabbath and Jubilee.

Distinctive Features. Though Leviticus contains mainly laws, some pieces of narrative are interspersed. The whole book is in the form of speeches delivered from the LORD to Moses, and, in this way, Leviticus joins the continuous story from Exodus to Numbers. Numerous concluding summaries help us understand the way the book is organized. The repeated explanations of individual laws, which often follow the conjunction "for," clarify the rationale for the laws. The various recurrent phrases are also worthy of note, particularly the phrase "I am the LORD your God," which sets the laws in the context of the first commandment.

Central Themes. Two underlying perceptions of the world stand behind Leviticus. On the one hand, the world created by God is ordered and good, as seen in Genesis 1. On the other hand, the world is a dangerous place because human beings can so easily disrupt the order, sin against God, and thus defile themselves, the community, and the world. The law is a gift from the Holy LORD to protect people and enable them to sustain and restore the order of the world when it is disrupted. The law provides for people a means by which they can make atonement, receive forgiveness, and maintain the wholeness and holiness of the community. To follow these laws is to be set apart as a people of God and to insure that all aspects of life are oriented to living life in the presence of the LORD.

NUMBERS

Historical Background and Authors. Numbers contains accounts of the second of two periods of wilderness wanderings (the first period was described in Exodus 13–18). Numbers, like Genesis and Exodus, contains a mixture of writings from J, E, and P (see "The Pentateuch," pp. 12-14). It covers the forty years of wandering in the wilderness from the departure from Sinai to the entry into the promised land.

Contents. Numbers moves from one generation that had trouble believing the promises of God, and thus died off, to a new generation that took its place. The first ten chapters of the book begin optimistically with a census of the Sinai generation (hence the title of the book, Numbers); a continuation of the giving of laws concerning rituals, purity, blessing, and offerings; and the beginning of a triumphant march to the promised land. Then comes a terrible period of rebellion or "murmuring" by the people (chaps. 11–25), which includes: rejecting the manna and craving meat, demanding water, revolting against and among the chosen leaders, and, most significantly, lacking faith in God's promise of land, a promise repeated through new victories and particularly through the miraculous oracles given by the prophet Balaam (chaps. 22–24). The people's lack of faith centers around the abortive attempt to enter the promised land in which twelve men went up to spy on Canaan, but only Joshua and Caleb believed that the battle against the inhabitants would be successful. Because of this lack of trust, the Israelites were confined to the desert and not permitted to enter Canaan until that generation died. The last chapters, which open with a census of the new generation (chap. 26), contain renewed laws and significant issues of division of the land and end with the new generation poised at the edge of the promised land.

Distinctive Features. Numbers contains various types of literature including censuses, itineraries, laws, lists, ancient poetry in the Balaam cycle, and various stories of conquest and rebellion.

Numbers also provides stories about Moses, now a mature leader who acts as judge and mediator. Many of the accounts center on leadership conflicts within the community involving priests, prophets, elders, and others, notably Miriam and Aaron.

Central Themes. Two themes dominate Numbers: the Lord's miraculous care for and guidance of Israel, and the people's willful resistance, ingratitude, rebellion, and lack of faith. Numbers portrays a period of testing, isolation, and radical dependence in which relationships with the LORD and the organization of the community are honed. From Numbers we learn that in the midst of disobedience, punishment, divine anger, and even death, God's promise of land and children holds fast.

DEUTERONOMY

Author and Historical Background. Deuteronomy, or "second law," is the second of the two law books in the Pentateuch (Leviticus is the first). The core of Deuteronomy is possibly the "book of the law" which was discovered when Josiah repaired the temple of Jerusalem in 621 B.C. This book provided the backbone for Josiah's reforms in the south (see 2 Kings 22–23). The original book gradually expanded to meet the demands of changing times and finally reflects the exilic concerns of the Deuteronomist (D) who combined insights from the Northern prophets, Southern Levites, and wisdom circles with the principles of the original Mosaic law (see "The Pentateuch").

Contents. Deuteronomy is presented as the final speeches of Moses to his people as they look forward to entering the promised land. The book begins with reminders and retellings of God's past actions (chaps. 1–4). The heart of the book (chaps. 4–26) contains a series of laws dealing with such matters as worshiping one God in one place, caring for the land, kingship, priesthood, family life, holy war, true and false prophecy, and tithing. These laws begin with a renewed presentation of the Ten Commandments and the giving of the central proclamation of Jewish religious life (called the *Shema,* meaning "Hear, O Israel," 6:4-9)

21

and end with a liturgical creed (26:5-10). Deuteronomy then describes two covenant ceremonies that include a series of blessings and curses, both of which reaffirm the Mosaic covenant (chaps. 27–30). The book ends with the song, blessing, and death of Moses (chaps. 31–34).

Distinctive Features. Deuteronomy is filled with dynamic, persuasive speech, calling on the people to live lives devoted to God and obedient to the law so that it might go well with them in the promised land. Deuteronomy can be read as an expanded covenant treaty between two parties—one, the LORD, and the other, Israel. The LORD, for his part, has in the past delivered Israel from slavery, led them through the wilderness, and promises to care for them in the good and fruitful land which lies before them. Israel, for her part, promises to love, serve, and obey God and to keep God's law. The lists of blessings and curses mark the consequences of obedience or disobedience.

Central Themes. Deuteronomy, the book most quoted by Jesus, captures for us the compelling nature and central spirit of the law. Whereas in Leviticus the motivation for keeping the law was maintaining holiness, in Deuteronomy the great love of God for his people makes clear the urgent need for all people individually, past and present, to respond by loving both God and neighbor. Israel is to respond both because she has been chosen and saved and also in order that life in Canaan might be peaceful and just. Among the laws the most pressing concerns include the unity of worship—the one people shall worship the one true God in one place—maintenance of the community and its traditions, and deep social concerns based on principles of equity, just use of power and riches, and protection of the poor and needy.

Place in the Canon. The importance of Deuteronomy cannot be overestimated as this book holds two significant places in the Old Testament: it is both the last book of the Pentateuch and the opening book of the early history books (see next section). By ending the Pentateuch with Deuteronomy, with Israel poised on the edge of the promised land, rather than after Joshua and entry into the land, these most holy books do not look to God solely on the basis of things he has already given. Instead, the Pentateuch, as the word of God for us, finally emphasizes being sustained primarily by the promise of the LORD, ever hopeful and ever looking toward the future.

The Historical Books

The twelve historical books—Joshua, Judges, Ruth, 1 and 2 Samuel, 1 and 2 Kings, 1 and 2 Chronicles, Ezra, Nehemiah, and Esther—are best divided into two groups.

Joshua through Kings, except for Ruth, form part of the Deuteronomistic history in which the principles espoused in Deuteronomy become the key principles used to interpret history. They cover the period of history from the days of Israel's judges (1200–1000 B.C.) through the kings up to the Babylonian exile (586). These books, which gather up traditions and stories from different centuries and places, were edited finally from the perspective of the exile. The final writers/compilers looked at their present situation and asked two questions: What went wrong? and Is there hope for the future?

Regarding the first question, the people of Israel looked back over their history to seek an explanation for the defeat by the enemy and the exile into Babylon. Did not God promise to be with Israel and protect the land and their temple? Why did Babylon win? The books from Joshua to Kings suggest that the exile came as God's punishment because the people did not fulfill their part of the covenant spelled out so clearly in Deuteronomy. The people did not love and serve God and did not listen to the words of the prophets. Regarding the second question, the people looked forward in the midst of exile, asking what they should do now. The answer: Repent and trust in the LORD who has never failed them.

In Jewish tradition, Joshua through Kings, minus Ruth, are identified as the early prophets (or former prophets) because the material deals as much with prophetic figures as with kings and other leaders. From both Jewish and Christian perspectives, the whole section can be read as the story of the working out in history of God's prophetic word of demand and promise.

The second block of material from Chronicles through Esther covers the same period of time as Genesis through Kings but then continues from the return from exile and into the Persian period (538–333). This material examines the history from the perspective of later times, probably the fifth and fourth centuries. Considerable debate exists as to whether these books form one major unit, the work of the Chronicler, or two units in which Ezra and Nehemiah come from separate authors and times. In either case, the mood of these books is far more optimistic than the earlier history. The concerns center on worship and the temple, the faithfulness and purity of the people, and the positive leadership of the Davidic kings.

The whole history from Joshua on is punctuated by two independent short books, Ruth and Esther, which deal with the valor and contribution of individual heroic women.

Joshua

Historical Background and Geography. Joshua begins "after the death of Moses" and describes the Israelite conquest of Canaan. Most of the action in the early part of the book, until the battles in 10:28—11:23, takes place only in the territory of the tribe of Benjamin in such cities as Jericho, Gilgal, Ai, and Gibeah. For this reason some scholars suggest that traditions derived largely from the single tribe of Benjamin were later expanded and generalized to become the book of Joshua.

Contents. Joshua contains numerous tales of conquest. The most elaborate story recounts the fall of Jericho (chaps. 1–6) with accounts of Rahab and the spies, the crossing of the river Jordan with the ark, the meeting between Joshua and the LORD's commander, and the collapse of Jericho's walls. All of these parts are intermingled with hints of later festive, liturgical, and ritual celebrations. Other stories (chaps. 7–11) center around the defeat of Ai, the treaty with the Gibeonites, the battle with five kings, and the generalized capture of the south and north. Joshua contains a number of lists which enumerate defeated kings (chap. 12), the allotment and distribution of the land to the various tribes (chaps. 13–19), and cities of refuge and Levite cities (chaps. 20–21). The last three chapters describe some tribal homecomings, Joshua's final speech, a covenant ceremony at Shechem (chap. 24), and reports of the burials of Joshua, Joseph, and Aaron's son Eleazar.

Distinctive Features. The individual accounts in Joshua are marked by significant speeches by God and various leaders including Joshua, Rahab, and various officers. These speeches are reminiscent of the speeches of Moses in Deuteronomy in that they stress what God has done, God's power and promise of land, and the necessity of Israel's faithfulness and obedience. Though the figure of Joshua, who is depicted as servant, mediator, and military leader, holds an important place in the book, his portrayal remains far more elusive and wooden than that of Moses.

Central Themes. In Joshua the LORD is pictured as a holy warrior, fighting on the side of his people Israel against the peoples of Canaan who worship other gods. The theme of holy war, which includes disturbing aspects like the command to destroy all living things among the enemy, remains difficult for us to reconcile with other loving, just, and gracious aspects of God. This theme is presented in the context of both the judgment of God and the mystery of the election. The conquest of the land is something God does for the people. Hence, one finds a stress on the ark in battle as a symbol of divine presence. The book of Joshua is clearly a part of the Deuteronomistic history because it centers on God's promise, God's gracious gift of the land, the making of the covenant, and the necessity of serving and worshiping the LORD alone.

JUDGES

Historical Background. The book of Judges, which begins "after the death of Joshua," in some ways stands in contrast to the previous book. In Joshua Israel conquers all or most of the land, whereas in Judges the stress lies on Israel's inability to drive out the inhabitants. Judges suggests an underlying history of a more gradual settlement, tribe by tribe, over a number of centuries.

Contents. Judges tells a series of earthy, colorful accounts of different judges. These accounts are interspersed with notices of other known judges. A "judge" can be a type of governor, a military commander, or a charismatic leader. After a general introduction, Judges begins with stories of effective judges such as Othniel, Ehud, and especially Deborah, whose song (chap. 5) is one of the oldest literary pieces in Scripture. The book continues with tales of Gideon (chaps. 6–8), his son Abimelech (chap. 9), and Jephthah (chaps. 10–12), each with a problem or flaw in his character. Judges moves then to Samson (chaps. 13–16), an ignoble character who thought only of himself and yet was used by God to defeat the Philistines. The book ends with disturbing tales of Micah and the sanctuary at Dan (chaps. 17–18), a violent Levite, his concubine, and the subsequent sins of the tribe of Benjamin (chaps. 19–21). These last chapters, which tell of the disintegration of morality and society in Israel, are marked by the repeated phrase, "In those days, there was no king in Israel; all the people did what was right in their own eyes" (21:25).

Distinctive Features. Judges contains many older stories from the period of the settlement; each story easily might have stood originally on its own. The individual accounts are linked together in a Deuteronomistic pattern described most clearly in 2:11-23. According to this pattern, Israel, after a period of rest, does evil by serving other gods and forsaking the Lord. The Lord in anger raises up enemies who march against Israel. The people then cry out, and the Lord, moved by pity, raises up a judge who eventually saves the people. After a period of rest, the pattern resumes.

Central Themes. As with most of Deuteronomistic history, stress falls on the contrast between God's grace and the people's lack of faith. Interestingly, the movement from Israel as a faithful respondent to an Israel whose behavior is immoral and whose society has disintegrated is reflected in Judges in the stories about women. The first woman is Deborah, judge and prophetess; next comes Jephthah's daughter, tragic but noble; and the book ends with the concubine and other women who become victims of violence. As the women go, so goes all of Israel. Judges as a whole presses forward the growing need for moral and spiritual leadership. The response to this need would be provided by David and his royal line.

RUTH

Authorship and Place in the Canon. Ruth is an independent narrative which might have been written any time from David's reign to postexilic times. The author might have been a village priest, an elder, or a wise woman who told stories to edify the people. In the Jewish canon Ruth comes after Proverbs, whose final chapter describes the "woman of worth." In the Christian canon Ruth, which begins "in the days of the judges" and ends with the mention of David, provides a transition from the problem period of the judges to the promised era of the kings.

Contents. The book of Ruth actually revolves around the character of Naomi, who in the first chapter traveled with her family from Bethlehem to Moab and there lost her husband and two sons. Naomi returned—defeated, lonely, and angry with God—accompanied only by Ruth, her Moabite daughter-in-law. The book tells of her journey from this depression back to renewed hope in God, love of family, and a significant place in Israel's history. Ruth, the second major character of the book, is a woman of commitment and daring who left her family and country to

27

support Naomi. She endured difficult work in the fields (chap. 2) and risked rejection, public censure, and personal disaster (chap. 3) in order to live up to her commitment to her mother-in-law. The third principal character is Boaz, a man of value and cleverness, who recognized both Ruth's worth and his own responsibilities to Naomi as her next of kin.

Distinctive Features. The book of Ruth, like so many of the narratives in Genesis through Kings, uses action, suspense, humor, irony, and an acute sense of human character to illustrate the importance of faithfulness. In Ruth God works behind the scenes, indirectly active but mentioned only in the speeches of various people. Ruth's oath of loyalty and commitment in chapter 1 continues to be a crucial passage, in our tradition, to express familial commitment.

Central Themes. The book of Ruth explores the theme of loyalty and commitment in the context of individual and family relationships. The book shows us that what constitutes family is not necessarily determined by blood relationships. Things are not always what they seem. On the surface Ruth is no more than a foreign woman from the despised country of Moab. Yet Naomi, Boaz, and eventually their whole community recognize Ruth as a member of Naomi's family, thus insuring the subsequent blessings of marriage and the birth of Ruth's child, Obed. (Obed becomes the grandfather of David, Israel's principal king and the ancestor of the Messiah.) In stark contrast to Judges, the book moves from famine to harvest, emptiness to fullness, death to life. The individuals in the book of Ruth express to one another loyalty and goodness. Together two women and one man, linked by bonds of affection and commitment, change the course of history.

1 AND 2 SAMUEL

Historical Background and Authorship. The books of Samuel cover the period from the end of the days of the judges to the first days of the monarchy. Saul ruled somewhere in the period between 1050 and 1000 B.C. and David was king from 1000 to 962. Some scholars have identified two major sources which stand behind these books: an earlier source which favors kingship, written during the reign of Solomon (962–922), and a later source, dating from 750–650, which opposes kingship. In all probability, the literary history behind these books is more complicated and revolves around different cycles which tell about Samuel, Saul, and David. During the exile, the Deuteronomistic editors adapted the books and molded them so that they became part of the larger Deuteronomistic history.

Contents. The books of Samuel tell the overlapping stories of the lives of three principal characters: Samuel, Saul, and David. Samuel, judge and prophet, dominates 1 Samuel 1–12. These chapters tell of Samuel's birth and his tutelage under the high priest Eli, his activity as a judge (chap. 7), his choosing and anointing Saul king despite his own warnings against the abuses of kingship (chaps. 8–11), and his farewell address (chap. 12).

Saul, whose story is told largely in 1 Samuel 13–31, is one of the most tragic figures in the Old Testament. On the one hand, he is chosen by God to be king over all of Israel. On the other hand, because of Saul's disobedience (chaps. 13, 15), he is rejected by God and stripped of his kingship. Saul's plight is revealed through accounts of his battles with the Philistines (chaps. 13–15), his violent jealousy of his musician and servant, David, who is favored not only by God but even by his son, Jonathan, and his daughter, Michal (chaps. 16–27), and his grasping at kingship through a visit to the woman at Endor (chap. 28). In the end Saul lost his wits, his kingship, and his life (chap. 31).

David, the third major character, appears first in 1 Samuel where he is Saul's servant. David is there portrayed as a young man chosen from among his brothers and anointed by Samuel (chap. 16), victorious among the Philistines, especially in slaying Goliath (chap. 17), and accumulating power and admirers, always in conflict with Saul. Second Samuel begins after the death of

Saul and tells the story of David's kingship. The book begins with accounts in which David consolidated his power (chaps. 1–8) and was promised everlasting kingship by the LORD (chap. 7). Second Samuel 9–20 (with 1 Kings 1–2) provides a remarkable account of the court history of David. While on a national scale the emphasis falls on the issue of succession, these chapters are filled with gritty, human narratives, including accounts of David's adultery, murder, and repentance (chaps. 11–12), the rape of his daughter Tamar by his son Amnon (chap. 13), David's love for and struggle with his son Absalom who rebels against him (chaps. 13–19), and various other conflicts. Interspersed in these books are stories about Hannah and her son and Eli and his sons (1 Sam. 1–4), a narrative about the ark (1 Sam. 4–6; 2 Sam. 6), and appendices (2 Sam. 21–24) which include songs of David and an account of a census.

Distinctive Features. The books of Samuel are most remarkable for what they are not. They are not stories that simply glorify or idealize great leaders of the past. Rather, these books offer portraits of real people whose struggles, sins, and triumphs are woven into a history of a people being led by God. The stories are told with consummate skill and multiple layers of meaning and insight that invite each new generation of readers into the thoughts and motivations of the various characters.

The books of Samuel recount the beginning of prophecy as well as of kingship and depict the tasks of prophets in relation to kings throughout Israel's history: First, prophets anoint kings so that all may know that kingship comes from God. Thus Samuel anointed both Saul and David. Second, prophets deliver promises to kings as Nathan did in 2 Samuel 7. Third, prophets rebuke and judge kings and deliver to them the word of God. Thus Samuel rebuked Saul, and Nathan chastised David for his sinfulness against God in his dealings with Bathsheba and Uriah. Finally, prophets offer to kings God's forgiveness as Nathan did to David following David's repentance.

Central Themes. In 1 and 2 Samuel, family tensions intersect with national tensions. Tensions exist between those with power and those with none, between those chosen by God and those who assume their power and position through heredity. These themes are set right at the beginning: poor blind Eli, the priest who is unable to hear the word of God and whose sons are corrupt, is set over against Hannah, the once-barren mother. Hannah knows that her child, Samuel—the one who hears and is faithful to the call of God—is a gift of God. With a thanksgiving song that sings the themes of God's reign and provides the prototype of Mary's magnificat in Luke 2 of the New Testament, she gives up her child into the service of the LORD. The events of 1 Samuel move slowly, under God's watchful eye, toward David's kingship.

The central theme of these books revolves around issues and questions of leadership: Who should rule Israel, and how should they rule? Human kingship is viewed from the perspective that the LORD is the true king of Israel. Any human king must therefore serve the LORD. Moreover, God alone is able to choose a king, and God finally chooses David. God thus stands behind the establishment of David's line in the hope that this kingship will be ruled justly and in the fear of the LORD (see David's final words in 2 Samuel 23). Such hopes are not always realized. Even the chosen King David falters, gratifying his own needs and wishes. The choice of David is permanently sealed by covenant in 2 Samuel 7. Here the LORD makes an enduring promise that he will be with David and his seed forever. Here are the roots of the promise of a future Messiah. Through this means God promises to be with all of Israel and beyond.

1 AND 2 KINGS

Historical Background. The books of Kings begin with the death of David and reign of Solomon (962–922 B.C.) and move through the days of the divided kingdom until the fall of the North (722–721) and then the South (587–586). Tensions always existed between the Northern Kingdom, Israel, and the Southern Kingdom, Judah. ("Israel" sometimes refers to the whole kingdom but more often refers only to the North.) David and Solomon were both identified more with Judah than with the North. As soon as Solomon died, the North rebelled and set up its own kingdom. The history that stands behind these books is really two histories: one of Judah where the Davidic dynasty remained stable and the other of Israel where eight different dynasties reigned in its two-hundred-year existence. Various sources stand behind these books including: royal archives, annals, and prophetic narratives, notably the Northern Elijah-Elisha cycle (1 Kings 17—2 Kings 10). Finally the whole history is told from a Southern perspective in which kings from the North are always pictured in a negative light.

Contents. These books contain stories of kings and prophets. First Kings begins with a description of the transfer of power from David to Solomon (chaps. 1–2). First Kings 3–11 deals with Solomon's reign and emphasizes his wealth, wisdom, administrative skills, and particularly his building of the temple. At Solomon's death, the Northern tribes rebelled under Jeroboam I (922–901). The prophet Ahijah condemned Jeroboam for setting up golden calves in rival sanctuaries at Dan and Bethel (chaps. 12–14). Jeroboam's son was killed by a usurper, Baasha, whose son was then killed by Zimri, who was killed in turn by Omri. Omri (876–869), who founded a stable and powerful dynasty in Israel, is noted only for building the capital city, Samaria (16:23–28).

The principal stories about the North center around Omri's son, Ahab (869–851), Jezebel who was Ahab's wife, and the prophets Elijah and Elisha. Ahab and Jezebel are seen as quintessentially evil in their worship of Baal, rejection of God and his prophets, and their unjust and selfish style of leadership. The stories about Elijah include his reviving a widow's child, a contest with the prophets of Baal, a journey to Mount Carmel, condemnation of Ahab for taking Naboth's vineyard, ascension into heaven, and the call of his successor, Elisha (1 Kings 17—2 Kings 2).

Elisha, for his part, also revives a widow's son, cures a foreigner of leprosy, blinds the Syrian army, and stands behind Jehu's revolt (2 Kings 3–10). Jehu's bloody revolution brings an end to all the house of Ahab as predicted in 2 Kings 9.

Second Kings continues with descriptions of the kings of Judah and the final kings of Israel. The kings in Jehu's dynasty, which lasts for almost a century, and the usurpers who follow in quick succession are again condemned. The final years of confusion end with defeat by Assyria and permanent exile for the ten tribes of Israel.

The stories about the kings of Judah begin with Rehoboam, Solomon's headstrong son, who alienated the Northern tribes (1 Kings 12) and began a succession of Davidic kings who ruled only in Judah. These kings are variously condemned and admired. The rulers most strongly condemned are Ahaziah and his mother Athaliah (842–837), Amaziah (800–783), Ahaz (735–715), and, principally, Manasseh (697–642). The kings who are positively evaluated are Asa (913–873), Jehoshaphat (873–849), in part Joash (837–800), Uzziah (783–742), Hezekiah (727–698), and Josiah (640–609). Highlighted are these last two kings who learned the appropriate lessons from the fall of the North and went about reforming the kingdom of Judah. Hezekiah, through his faith and righteous actions and guided by the prophet Isaiah, turned back the Assyrians at the very walls of Jerusalem and miraculously recovered from a fatal illness (2 Kings 18–20). Josiah, for his part, repaired the Jerusalem temple and instituted numerous national and religious reforms on the basis of the "book of the law" (2 Kings 22–23; see also the historical background for Deuteronomy, p. 21). Despite their efforts, the terrible sins of Manasseh could not be overcome. Judah at last was defeated by the Babylonians; the temple lay in ruins; and the people were exiled to a foreign land. The book ends ironically with the Davidic king, Jehoiachin, sitting in exile at the table of the Babylonian king.

Distinctive Features. The books of Kings are marked by repeated summaries that coordinate the history and pass appropriate judgments. These judgments center around apostasy and improper worship. One principal sin is worshiping false gods. Particularly heinous is the worship of Ba'al, the major crime of Jezebel, but even Solomon is condemned for the behavior of his wives who worshiped foreign gods. The other principal sin involves worshiping the right God in the wrong way. The only true center of worship is Jerusalem. Thus special censure is given to Jeroboam when he rebelled against the South because he established the Northern cities of Dan and Bethel as worship centers. This "sin of Jeroboam" is subsequently committed by every Northern king. In the South, prior to Hezekiah, some worship was conducted outside of Jerusalem at the hilltop shrines or "high places." These practices, alongside of idol worship, setting up pillars, and various other abuses, are also condemned.

Central Themes. The books of Kings form the core of the Deuteronomistic history that was written to make sense of the exile, to teach people the errors of their ways, and to give some guidance and hope (see "The Historical Books," p. 23). In these books whatever God says comes to pass. Through interweaving the accounts of kings and prophets, history is shown to be guided by the word of God. The behavior of the kings affects the outcome of history. Exile is shown to have resulted from sin against God. The LORD did not lose to the gods of Assyria and Babylon. The LORD was and is in control. The people in exile can repent and turn from their own wayward paths. Finally their hope, as ours, lies in the assurance that the LORD's promise will outlast his just punishments.

1 AND 2 CHRONICLES

Date and Authorship. The books of Chronicles, which begin at creation and end with the edict of Cyrus (538 B.C.), were written sometime during the era of Persian rule (538–333), probably around 400, though scholars have suggested dates as early as 515 and as late as 250. Given the concern for Levites and singers, the author might possibly have belonged to one of these groups.

Contents. Much of Chronicles duplicates material from Samuel and Kings. However, major omissions, additions, and numerous subtle changes contribute to making Chronicles quite different in tone and effect. First Chronicles begins with an introduction (1 Chron. 1–9) which includes both genealogies and various lists of tribes, Jerusalemites, Levites, and others. The largest portion of Chronicles is devoted to David (1 Chron. 10–29) and Solomon (2 Chron. 1–9), both of whom are portrayed as nearly flawless. David is idealized as the king of all Israel, recipient of the promise, and planner of the temple and its personnel. Items omitted about David include the entire account of his rise to power, most of his dealings with Saul, his affair with Bathsheba and murder of Uriah, all family tension, and any reference to a struggle over succession. In the stories about Solomon, no reference is made to the difficulties at the beginning and end of his life. Emphasis is placed instead on his united reign, his great wealth, and especially his building of the temple.

The rest of Chronicles (2 Chron. 10–36) largely retells the history of the kings of Judah found in 1 and 2 Kings. The accounts and notices of the kings of Israel, the Northern Kingdom, are omitted entirely. Some lesser omissions and additions also have a noticeable effect. Chronicles offers some differences in judgments about various kings. For example, Rehoboam is not held responsible for the secession of the North and is judged both faithful and unfaithful; Abijah and Asa are viewed more negatively; the material about Jehoshaphat is expanded; and Manasseh, despite his overall wickedness, does repent. The major hero, after David and Solomon, is Hezekiah (2 Chron. 29–32). Portrayed as a new David and a new Solomon, Hezekiah resanctified the temple, celebrated Passover anew, and instituted general religious reforms. The final verses of Chronicles describe a seventy-year Sabbath rest for the land and the subsequent decree by Cyrus, the Persian king, who was moved by the LORD to announce the necessity of rebuilding the temple.

Distinctive Features. Much of the chronicler's distinctiveness is located in the material that is added to Samuel and Kings including: new speeches and prayers said by various characters; lists of personnel, especially Levites; new details about the planning and building of the temple; much mention of festivals and celebrations, especially Passover; and general attention to music and song. The division between the North and the South is barely acknowledged. Instead, considerable interest is given to the whole people who are idealized and spoken of as "all Israel." The continuity with "all Israel" is expressed both in the introductory chapters and also by various indications that Northerners are to be welcomed so long as they truly repent and accept the temple of Jerusalem.

Central Themes. The legitimacy and centrality of both the temple and the Davidic line dominate these two books. The chronicler affirms the stability, permanence, and continuity of kingship and temple. Given the lack of a contemporary Davidic king, the promise to David might, to a degree, be interpreted messianically. Theologically, great stress is given both to God's constant care and also to God's immediate and just retribution. This latter message is delivered particularly by prophets. People get precisely what they deserve. The kings who seek God and repent of their sins prosper; those who forsake the LORD are punished. Individual repentance is demanded. Hope is centered in the strong and permanent relationship between God and the people as experienced in the temple.

EZRA AND NEHEMIAH

Historical Background and Date. Ezra and Nehemiah, like the books before them, were originally one unit. The history behind these books is notoriously difficult to sort out, even to the point of not knowing for certain whether Ezra, the priest and scribe, preceded Nehemiah, the governor. Both books tell of the period of restoration in Jerusalem after the Babylonian exile. Most scholars place Ezra before Nehemiah during the realm of the Persian King Artaxerxes I (465–424 B.C.). The identity of the author is equally unclear. Many have suggested that these books were written by the author of 1 and 2 Chronicles. However, because of differences in emphases and theme, others have suggested a separate author who, sometime later in the Persian Era, combined and reworked the memoirs of Ezra and Nehemiah.

Contents. Ezra and Nehemiah are easily divided into four sections. Each section has a recurrent pattern in which: God moves the heart of the Persian king; something is built; the project meets with opposition; and through God's help, the opposition is overcome.

The first section, Ezra 1–6, deals with the return from Babylon and the rebuilding of the temple under the leadership of Zerubbabel. This section includes lists of those who returned, accounts of the reestablishment of the altar, and various details of the rebuilding of the temple. Resistance was offered by "the people of the land," who stop the project and exchange various letters with the rulers of the land. Despite their objections, the temple was finally rebuilt and dedicated, and Passover was duly celebrated.

The second section, Ezra 7–10, deals with rebuilding the community under the leadership of Ezra, a scribe and priestly descendent of Aaron. Ezra led a group of lay people and priests in an elaborate trip back from Babylon with various gifts for the temple. Ezra's major intent centered on reinstituting the law of Moses. This intent entailed disbanding the numerous interreligious marriages between the Jews and Gentiles which, according to Ezra, violated the commandments of the prophets. Over some objection, the foreign wives and children were expelled.

The third section, Nehemiah 1–7, deals with rebuilding the walls of Jerusalem under the leadership of Nehemiah, who brought home a new group of exiles. The opposition was led by

Sanballat, governor of Samaria, and others. Despite obstacles, which included ridicule, threat of violence, and economic difficulties, the wall was rebuilt.

The final section includes the climactic reading of "the book of the law of Moses" by Ezra (Neh. 8–10) and some additional acts of Nehemiah (Neh. 11–13). The book of the law was likely an early version of the Pentateuch. The public reading produced joy and weeping in the people. Under Ezra's leadership, they also celebrated the Feast of Booths and initiated a day of mourning, a confession, and a renewed covenant to keep God's law. This reading of the law and the people's response constituted the principal act which solidified the postexilic community, now renewed and purified in celebration and in covenant faith.

Distinctive Features. Ezra and Nehemiah are marked by a strong sense of religious mission on the part of the Jews returning from exile. The mission was conducted under the auspices of God in the spirit of repentance and rejoicing. Unlike Chronicles, these books show no interest at all in David and his descendants. Historical memory centers on the figure of Moses and experiences of the Exodus, wilderness, and conquest, particularly in Ezra's confession in Nehemiah 9. Ezra is himself portrayed as a new Moses.

Central Themes. Ezra and Nehemiah center around concerns for the temple, the purified community, the city of Jerusalem, and the law. Unbroken continuity with the old Mosaic law and the first temple are exceedingly important. Concern for the purity of the community necessitated a strict forbiddance of intermarriage in order to prevent syncretism or "pollution" by the "peoples of the land." Emphasis is placed on hearing and obeying the law. The Jewish people responded with repentance and celebration showing that one can be faithful even under foreign rule.

ESTHER

Historical Background, Date, Author, and Purpose. The book of Esther is set in the Persian court of Xerxes I (486–465

B.C.), who is called by the name Ahasuerus in Esther, Ezra, and Daniel. The book itself was written sometime later, perhaps during a time of Jewish persecution. Esther was written to comfort, inspire, and uplift the Jews who had been scattered during the exiles, to assure them of the importance of their survival, and to undergird and legitimate the festival of Purim.

Contents.   Esther tells the story of King Ahasuerus, his Queen Esther, her cousin and guardian, Mordecai, and the wicked prime minister, Haman. The book begins at the court of Ahasuerus at a time when he was married to the beautiful Vashti. When Vashti refused to appear as commanded before the king, he ordered her banished and instituted a search for a new queen. Ahasuerus found and married Esther, a beautiful Jewish maiden, whose cousin Mordecai was an officer of the court. When Mordecai, a pious Jew, refused to bow down to Haman, Haman responded by convincing the king to have Mordecai hanged and all Jews killed. Esther, through a clever plot and with considerable bravery, tricked Haman into revealing his wickedness before the king. She thus saved both her cousin and her people. In the end of the book, in place of the expected destruction of the Jews, King Ahasuerus ordered the execution of Haman and all the other enemies of the Jews, and the festival of Purim was instituted to celebrate the victory.

Distinctive Features.   The book of Esther, one of Scripture's main heroic legends, contains numerous exaggerations—the women are the most beautiful, Haman the most wicked, and so forth. The characters and the numbers are inflated, and the story is filled with reversals and ironies. Esther is often noted as the only book in Scripture in which God is never mentioned. This absence was early remedied by the additions of prayers, letters, and dreams in the Greek and Latin versions of Esther which are listed as the "Additions to Esther" in the Apocrypha.

Central Themes.   On one level, the principal theme of Esther is the celebration of Purim. However, through its ironies and exaggerations, Esther also examines issues of the nature and abuse of power as well as the issue of God's indirect control of history. Despite the fact that God does not act directly in the book, God is shown to stand behind Esther's noble actions on behalf of her people in 4:14. This key speech of Mordecai to Esther captures the central theme of the book: "For if you keep silent at such a time as this, relief and deliverance will rise for the Jews from another quarter. . . . Who knows? Perhaps you have come to royal dignity for just such a time as this."

The Psalms and Wisdom Literature

The third group of writings in the Old Testament includes five diverse books: Job, Psalms, Proverbs, Ecclesiastes, and the Song of Solomon. The order in which these books appear is fairly flexible within the different traditions. In the Jewish canon these books, together with Ruth, Lamentations, Esther, Daniel, Ezra–Nehemiah, and 1 and 2 Chronicles, make up the third major portion of Scripture called the "Writings." The Writings were the last portion of Scripture to be included in the canon, and their inclusion may not have been totally settled until after the fall of the second temple in A.D. 70.

Because each of the five books has its own literary history and perspective, generalizations are not always helpful. Most of the writing is poetry as opposed to prose. The book of Psalms is comprised of diverse hymns and prayers of Israel from all periods of her history. Song of Solomon contains moving love poetry. The other three books, often identified as wisdom literature, are set apart by a number of individual traits. These books do not deal so much with the story and history of Israel, with laws, with covenant, or with revelation. Rather, the wisdom writings concentrate on issues and experiences of daily life, on learning how to live a good and productive life, and on exploring great philosophical questions such as the nature of good and evil, the righteousness of God, and the place and source of wisdom in our lives. These books were composed by Israel's wise people, who included both tribal leaders such as village elders and wise women, and professional sages such as royal counselors, scribes, and teachers.

JOB

Authorship and Date. The book of Job, one of the great philosophical books of Scripture, is notoriously difficult to date. The story takes place in a patriarchal setting in an unknown land at an unspecified ancient time. Most likely, given similarities to Jeremiah and Psalms and possible anti-Deuteronomistic sentiments, the book should be dated during the exilic or early post-exilic period. The author was clearly a sage given to pondering human problems.

Contents. The book of Job opens with a two-chapter prose narrative about a man named Job who was blameless and upright, and who feared, that is, loved and obeyed, God. He had a large family and many possessions. One day the Lord and a member of his heavenly council, Satan, were looking down on earth from heaven, and God commented to Satan as to Job's fine character. Thereupon Satan issued a challenge to God saying that if God were to take away Job's possessions, family, and eventually his health, then Job would curse rather than fear and love God. This God did, but Job, left to cry among the ashes with only his three friends to comfort him, did not curse God. After this introduction, the book continues with a long poetic dialogue between Job and his friends, which includes numerous laments, speeches, and disputations. Job lamented the day of his birth (chap. 3), complained about his unjust suffering, and called God to trial for punishing him even though he had been a good man. The three friends, Eliphaz, Bildad, and Zophar, who were eventually joined by a fourth friend, Elihu (chaps. 32–37), offered various misguided reasons why Job's punishment was deserved, such as: Job must have done something bad, all people sin, or suffering can be good. Eventually God appeared in a whirlwind and addressed Job directly by asking numerous questions about creation, care of the earth and its beasts, justice and nature, and Job's place in the universe (chaps. 38–41). Job then repented in dust and ashes. The book ends with a prose epilogue (chap. 42) in which God restored the fortunes of Job and gave him a new family.

Distinctive Features. Most distinctive is the combination in Job of story and poetry. The poetic dialogue within the prose account contains three cycles of questions and answers (though the third cycle is disrupted and irregular), Elihu's speeches, and God's response. The author probably started with an old legend and then adapted and expanded it by adding the internal poetic section. The various suggestions of the friends which stand in marked contrast to the continuous suffering of Job draw the reader ever deeper into the issues of suffering and the justice of God.

Central Themes. The book of Job helps its readers to struggle with two interwoven questions concerning justice and piety: Why do the innocent suffer? and Can we worship God freely, without wanting something in return? Behind these questions stands an examination of the assumption, based on older wisdom and perhaps Deuteronomistic philosophy, that the good are always rewarded and the bad always punished. God, from the whirlwind, suggests that this formula is mistaken, that God's ways are not so easily grasped. God, in his own unpredictable, powerful, and mysterious way, loves and cares for the world, the beasts, and Job.

PSALMS

Authorship and Date. The book of Psalms, or Psalter, contains one hundred fifty psalms from the worship life of ancient Israel. Traditionally David has been considered the author of the psalms, and many of the psalms are attributed to him or, at least, sung in his name. The Psalter contains some smaller collections such as the psalms of ascent, probably songs of pilgrims traveling up to Jerusalem, and the psalms of Asaph and Korah, which may originally have come from the Northern Kingdom. The Psalter is divided into five books, each possibly with its own history. Many of the psalms were originally associated with the temple at Jerusalem. These came from major celebrations or festivals, from national lament services, and from daily celebrations or festivals, from national lament services, and from daily sacrificial services. Some psalms may have been derived from home or synagogue worship.

Contents. Though the order and titles of the psalms may have some significance, more recently the psalms have been classified according to certain similarities of form and content. The most general categories include: *community songs of praise,* or *hymns,* which offer general praise of God as creator and redeemer (Pss. 8, 29, 33, 66, 103, 104, 113, 135, 145–150); *community laments,* or *supplications,* which often bemoan some defeat such as the fall of the temple or exile (Pss. 60, 74, 79, 80, 90, 137); *individual laments,* or prayers for help, whose very lack of specificity allows for flexibility in use (Pss. 3–7, 13, 22, 38–40, 53–57, 139–143); and *individual thanksgivings* (Pss. 23, 30, 63, 116, 138).

Other overlapping categories, often more dependent on content than form, include: *liturgies* (Pss. 24, 68, 100, 118, 132); *penitential psalms* (Pss. 6, 32, 38, 51, 102, 130, 143); *psalms of sacred history* in which the history of Israel is recited in the context of praise (Pss. 78, 105, 106); *psalms of blessing* (Pss. 91, 121, 127–128); *wisdom psalms* (Pss. 32, 34, 37, 111–112), especially Torah psalms which praise the law (Pss. 1, 19, 119); *songs of Zion* which often express a yearning for Jerusalem (Pss. 46, 48, 76, 84, 87, 122); *enthronement psalms* which sing to the LORD as king (Pss. 47, 93, 95–99); and *royal psalms* which originally extol the living kings of David's line but eventually take on a messianic and eschatological flavor (Pss. 2, 18, 45, 89, 110). (The psalms in parentheses are offered as examples and do not cover all psalms in the individual categories.)

Distinctive Features. Although the psalms can be grouped in general categories, each also has its own individual beauty and message. The poetry of the psalms centers around each parallel line where a thought, once said, is expanded, modified, or embellished in the second and, occasionally, third part of the line. The psalms make exquisite use of poetic devices such as metaphor, sound and word play, vivid imagery, repetition, and balanced structures called "chiasms" in which the end matches the beginning and the center is the point of emphasis, as in Psalms 8 and 103.

Central Themes. Together and individually, the psalms express the praise and glorification of God. Even in the laments, the assurance of divine presence makes it possible to cry out in complaint and sorrow. In the psalms, God is praised as Creator, as Lord of history and nature, and as Redeemer of individuals, of Israel, and of the world. God is portrayed as holy and loyal, powerful and compassionate, lordly and forgiving. The psalms convey a sense of human sin, hopelessness, and despair balanced with joy, adoration, and absolute dependence on the Almighty. The praises and laments of the psalms have become the universal Jewish and Christian language of prayer, filled with beauty and spiritual depth, teaching generations how to pray.

PROVERBS

Authorship and Date. The book of Proverbs, traditionally attributed to Solomon, the ideal wise king, actually comes from a variety of sources. Reflected in the book is wisdom from the clan, some school and scribal wisdom, and some wisdom from the royal court. Also notable are significant links with and dependence on international wisdom insofar as some of the material overlaps considerably with earlier Egyptian wisdom writing. The book, which possibly contains material from various periods of Israel's history, came to be in its final form after the exile.

Contents. The book of Proverbs is most easily divided into two major parts. Proverbs 1–9 contains: an introduction to the book (1:1-7), ten "instructions" with numerous admonitions and prohibitions about moral behavior often addressed to "my son," and several poems which describe the personified figure of Wisdom (1:20-33; 8) and contrast her with Folly (chap. 9). The description of Wisdom draws heavily on both prophetic and goddess imagery. She is said to have been beside the LORD in the ordering of creation, and she calls to humanity to keep her ways and thus find life.

The second part of Proverbs contains several collections made up mostly of individual two-part sentences, each called a proverb or "mashal." Each proverb offers a terse description or saying with an eye toward persuading the reader to new perspectives and morally upright action. These collections also contain several extended metaphors, "better than" and "happy is" sayings, and some similes or comparisons. Some of the recurrent themes, frequently set in contrast, include the importance of wisdom over folly, knowledge over ignorance, patience over impatience, well-informed speech over brashness, silence over gossip, diligence over laziness, wealth over poverty but integrity over falsehood, righteousness over violence, and love over hate. The book ends with the skeptical words of Agur, a collection of sayings based on numbers of things, the words of Lemuel, and an extended description of a woman of worth (chaps. 30–31).

Distinctive Features. Proverbs 1–9 sets the tone with a more philosophical, thorough, and prescriptive approach. Proverbs 10 and following, though made up more of individual proverbs, are not always randomly arranged. When read in context, the proverbs often inform each other and draw the reader into deliberation. Notable, for example, is Proverbs 26:4-5 where two contradictory proverbs stand next to each other. Thus the reader is invited to think about the situation, to consider the nature of wisdom, to agree and disagree, and to become genuinely involved with assessing the offered counsel.

Central Themes. The book of Proverbs is filled with advice and serious contemplations based on keen observation of the world. Proverbs thus combines a sort of scientific observation with poetic form. This combination is born of the conviction that true observations can only be expressed poetically and facts cannot be separated from values. The emphasis falls on finding and leading a good, productive, and satisfying life. Though decidedly not revealed law, Proverbs centers on the observation that the fear of the LORD is the beginning of wisdom. In reading Proverbs, one participates in the search for order and meaning. The figure of Wisdom, mentioned above, points to the discovery that the true order of creation comes from God, and, by attending to her voice, humans can share in Wisdom's bounty and goodness.

ECCLESIASTES

Authorship and Date. The book of Ecclesiastes, also known as Qohelet, possibly dates from as late as 300–200 B.C. Ecclesiastes, like Proverbs, is traditionally assigned to Solomon and is told from the perspective of an old king or sage. Within the book the author is referred to as "the preacher."

Contents. In Ecclesiastes the preacher looks back over his life and notes that all is vanity, or evaporating mist, and a striving after the wind. He explores many avenues of life, including pleasure, wisdom, and wealth, in an attempt to find meaning. What he discovers is that nothing new happens "under the sun," and human toil brings no gain. Much of his frustration comes from not knowing. In chapter 3 the preacher reasons that though there is a time for everything, humans cannot know this time; they cannot know the beginning and the end of things, and thus they live in frustration. The preacher further discovers that humans cannot know their own end, except that they will die just as the beast, and they cannot know what will come after. Mostly, the preacher finds that he cannot know the Creator, who is distant and detached. Through all this the preacher offers proverbial advice encouraging a certain detachment, keeping vows, and favoring moderation and wisdom. He counsels seven times that people eat, drink, and enjoy the good things of life that God gives them. The book ends with a moving description of aging (12:1-8) and an epilogue that commends the study of proverbs, fearing God, and keeping the commandments.

Distinctive Features. Ecclesiastes is the most philosophical of all the writings of Scripture, filled with sustained observations and reflections. The language of the book is unique, rife with repeated phrases, extended treatises, and random proverbs and sayings. Many readers have been confused by the seeming contradictions and lack of clear structure. Some have suggested the presence of numerous editors, while others suggest that the author frequently quoted certain proverbs in order to refute them.

Central Themes. Ecclesiastes shares with Job a skepticism of traditional answers which assume that good is rewarded and bad punished. Some readers see his thoughts as cynical and depressing, reflecting the preacher's crisis of faith and his calling into question all that came before. But Ecclesiastes can also be uplifting. The preacher concludes that once people discover that they cannot create their own meaning or know the truth behind all things, then they can leave such matters to God and learn to find pleasure in the simple living of life.

SONG OF SOLOMON

Authorship and Date. The final book traditionally assigned to Solomon is the Song of Solomon, also called the Song of Songs and Canticles. The author is unknown, and dating estimates have ranged from 950 B.C. to late postexilic times. While some have seen the Song as material from a royal or secular wedding, a sacred drama, or even from a fertility cult, most would identify it simply as love poetry.

Contents. The Song of Songs centers around two lovers—a "radiant and ruddy" young man and a "black and beautiful" young woman. They work as shepherds in the countryside and sing their undying love for each other in a series of monologues and dialogues. Alone, they are in paradise and celebrate their physical beauty and sexual pleasure. Other characters, however, do intrude. The daughters of Jerusalem bring in scorn and jealousy. The watchmen of the city, where the woman gets lost in her search for her lover, threaten violence and danger. The language of the song is evocative and sensual as the lovers, who address each other as "beloved," rejoice in their adoration of the other.

Distinctive Features. The Song of Solomon contains the most explicitly erotic poetry in Scripture. The unusual imagery and strong metaphors, the frequent anonymity of the speakers, and the forty-nine words which occur only in this book make the Song quite difficult to translate. The structure also offers a challenge. Some see the Song as a collection of individual poems, ranging in number from six to forty. Others read the Song as one long poem with various parts because of the frequent repetitions and interweaving phrases.

Central Themes. Discerning the central theme has been a challenge for both Jews and Christians down through the centuries. Most often the book has been interpreted metaphorically as a mystical allegory of the love between the Lord and Israel, Christ and the church, or God and the human soul. Recently the Song has been interpreted more literally as a celebration of innocent and physical love. The Song, with its many allusions to trees, fruit, and animals as well as frequent verbs of tasting, smelling, touching, seeing, and hearing, also has been read as a return to Eden and to sexuality as the Creator intended it to be. The two lovers together are strong, committed, mutual in their relationship, free of domination, at one with the natural world, and rejoicing always in the other.

The Prophets

The final group of books in the Old Testament is the prophetic books, which include the books of the three major prophets—

Isaiah, Jeremiah, and Ezekiel—the book of Daniel, a small book of Lamentations attached to Jeremiah, and a united collection of the twelve minor prophets. (The terms *major* and *minor* refer to length, not importance!) The Jewish canon differs only slightly in that Daniel and Lamentations are included in the Writings, and the prophets as a whole make up the second rather than the last section. The final version of the prophetic writings, except Daniel, was probably in place by around 180 B.C.

A prophet is a person called by God to deliver messages from God to the people. At times prophets also act as mediators to God on behalf of the people. Prophets can be isolated individuals, associated with a specific cultic center, or part of an itinerant group of prophets, as we learn from the accounts found in the historic books. The prophets whose writings make up these seventeen books represent only a small number of the prophets who spoke in ancient Israel. Not all prophetic messages were considered authentic.

While each of the prophetic books has its individual characteristics, certain similar features are worthy of note. At the heart of this material lies the prophetic word from God or "oracle" that was originally delivered orally. These oracles include (1) proclamations of judgment against Israel and/or Judah or against other nations, and (2) proclamations of salvation. Thus the prophets offer warning and condemnation on one hand, and hope and visions of the future on the other. These two central types of prophetic speech correspond to the two principal purposes of prophecy: to condemn people for injustice, disobedience, and refusal to obey or even to recognize God, and to give hope for the future and extend the promises of God toward the final consummation of history. Other modes of prophetic speech include woe sayings, songs, dirges, parables, and longer discourses.

The prophetic books also contain information about the prophets, given in both the first and third persons. Central to this biographical information is the "call narrative," found already in the historical books (1 Sam. 3; 1 Kings 22), which formally describes a prophet's call, complete with instructions, the prophet's personal objections, assurances of God's presence, and visions (Jer. 1, Isa. 6, Isa. 40). One also finds words the prophets address to God, such as lamentations and prayers, accounts of symbolic actions, and encounters with authorities. The prophetic books are written mostly in poetry with some intermittent prose. Prophetic language is sometimes violent, often visionary, and always reflects God's word to the people.

Much of the material in the prophetic books is original with the individual prophets; however, these books also include certain expanding and supplemental material. Introductions, secondary accounts, and hymns, as well as extra prophetic material presented as the words of the prophets, were added by different generations of believers. Some material was added by immediate disciples who collected, wrote down, and arranged the words of the prophets. This material was then often enlarged in different places and during subsequent eras. Many of the books are therefore repositories of generations of cumulative material expanding the word of God to speak to each new generation. The history of each book can be complicated and often is not easily deciphered.

The dates of the individual prophets will be given as each book is examined, but an overall chronological list as follows can also be helpful.

1. Eighth-century B.C. (800–700) prophets include Amos and Hosea, who spoke to the Northern Kingdom until its defeat by Assyria (722/721), and First Isaiah and Micah who spoke to the south.
2. Seventh-century (700–586) prophets include Jeremiah, Nahum, Habakkuk, and Zephaniah who spoke to Judah until its defeat by Babylon (587/586).
3. Exilic (586–538) prophets include Ezekiel and Second Isaiah.
4. Postexilic prophets during the rebuilding of the temple (515) include Haggai, Zechariah, and Third Isaiah.

5. Later postexilic prophets (500–400) include Joel, Obadiah, Jonah, and Malachi.
6. Daniel was written in the Hellenistic period (approximately 164 B.C.).

ISAIAH

Identity of Prophet and Date. The book of Isaiah has the most complex history of any of the prophetic books. Chapters 1–39 are the most closely identified with the eighth-century prophet Isaiah, sometimes called First Isaiah, who prophesied in Jerusalem to the Southern Kingdom of Judah during the reigns of Jotham, Ahaz, and Hezekiah (742–687). Little is known of Isaiah's personal life, though he may have had priestly connections. Chapters 1–39 were first expanded by the writings of an anonymous exilic prophet, often called Second Isaiah (chaps. 40–55), who announces the end of the exile (539). The final expansion (chaps. 56–66) comes from a third writer, Third Isaiah, who lived in Jerusalem during the rebuilding of the temple (538–510) and was probably a disciple of Second Isaiah.

Contents. Chapters 1–12 contain the bulk of the prophetic utterances of First Isaiah. These chapters begin with various prophetic judgments against Judah, first because of unrighteousness, social injustice, and rejection of the teachings of the holy LORD, and second because of outside alliances. These chapters include a moving song of the vineyard (chap. 5), Isaiah's call in the temple (chap. 6), and some profound visions of the future which center on hopes of a messianic king who will bring justice and harmony (2:1-4; 4:2-6; 7:14-16; 9:2-7; 11). Chapters 1–12 are followed by: oracles against the nations (chaps. 13–23); a small collection (chaps. 24–27) of later writings, called "Isaiah's apocalypse," which describe the final banquet, heavenly signs, and the like; various oracles against Judah, Assyria, and Egypt (chaps. 28–32); some later oracles about the end times (chaps. 33–35); and a historic appendix (chaps. 37–39) which largely

51

duplicates 2 Kings 18:13—20:19 and speaks of Isaiah's encounters with King Hezekiah.

Chapters 40–55 begin with a call to those in exile to comfort Israel and proclaim the release of the captives. This work of unparalleled poetic beauty continues with hymns to God—glorious king, creator of all things, redeemer and restorer of Israel—who holds idols in disdain and brings nations to judgment. Interspersed are four servant songs (42:1–4; 49:1–6; 50:4–11; 52:13—53:12) which speak of an individual, probably representing both all of Israel in general and a prophetic figure in particular. This servant takes on the suffering of the nations in order to bring Israel, and ultimately the nations, back to God.

The last chapters reflect a more complex national situation. The exiles were back home in Jerusalem and faced the task of living up to the demands of God's word and rebuilding the holy city. Third Isaiah contains oracles against corruption, idolatry, and injustice and in favor of the poor and the faithful. These chapters call for a divine judgment that will separate the righteous from the unrighteous, true Israel from false, and will bring light into the darkness. Third Isaiah both demands repentance and obedience to the commandments and offers consolation and hope for a restored Zion. In visions of the future, the LORD leads a great procession that includes the righteous among the nations (chap. 60) and creates a new heaven and a new earth (65:17–25) reminiscent of Isaiah 11.

Distinctive Features. Each of the three sections contributes its own individual features. First Isaiah, which speaks of the Holy One of Israel who stands over against a sinful people, moves roughly in chronological order through Isaiah's prophetic career, offering both judgment and hope. Second Isaiah makes great use of earlier hymnic and liturgical forms. Certain key ideas and phrases, such as emphasis on first and last things, the passing away of the old, God's doing a new thing, and the centrality of the word, are intertwined and repeated. Third Isaiah, heavily dependent on what comes before, recalls many of the judgments of First Isaiah, though the judgments become more intense. Third Isaiah also transforms the visions of Second Isaiah to a more apocalyptic projection; that is, hope is projected into the distant future of a new heaven and earth.

Central Themes. First Isaiah preaches absolute dependence on the LORD as opposed to foreign nations, alliances, and undeserving leaders. Social injustice indicates a lack of holiness and righteousness. Hope rests in God's holy mountain Jerusalem/Zion, in the Davidic king, and predominantly on the word of God which goes forth from Zion. As the present becomes more uncertain and punishment for iniquities becomes inevitable, hope becomes more oriented toward the future. Second Isaiah's message centers on the proclamation of good news to Israel, God's servant. The prophet portrays God as Creator, Redeemer, and Lord of all. Hope lies in the past, through creation and the exodus; the present, which is a time of a new exodus and a new creation; and the future, when the people will return from Babylonian exile to Jerusalem. Through exile, Israel has received her just punishment. But suffering has been redemptive, and Israel has received double for all her sins. Third Isaiah also looks to the future. The present is more difficult; the task of repentance and purification is not yet complete. The visions of the future carry terrible judgment and glorious promise not just for Israel but, through Zion, for all the nations.

The book of Isaiah moves from the holy city of Jerusalem to exile in Babylon and back again to Zion. It moves between judgment and comfort and contains words of vision and promise which have inspired Christian readers throughout the generations. With its all-encompassing scope, Isaiah calls on Israel and the church to be faithful to the past, to be repentant in the present, and to look hopefully to the future fulfillment of God's word.

JEREMIAH

Identity of Prophet and Date. Jeremiah prophesied in Jerusalem from 627–580 B.C. during the time of Josiah and the last reigning kings of Judah. His family, descendants of the deposed priestly line of Abiathar (2 Kings 2:26-27), lived in Anathoth, a small town only three miles from Jerusalem. More is known about Jeremiah than about any other prophetic figure, though the "facts" are not always clear. Jeremiah, whose message was unpopular and often met with hostility, interacted frequently with kings and other leaders. He spoke regularly of the exile in Babylon but was himself finally abducted to Egypt by his enemies.

Contents.   The book begins with God's call to Jeremiah when he was only a youth. In his prophetic oracles Jeremiah denounced Judah's apostasy, false worship such as idolatry and the worship of other gods, rejecting the law, breaking the covenant, and irresponsible dependence on the temple. Jeremiah particularly condemned the corrupt leadership of princes, priests, false prophets, elders, and sages, and he announced God's judgment on Judah through the coming of "the enemy from the north."

The oracles are supplemented by four additional types of material: prose sermons or speeches, symbolic actions, laments, and narrative accounts. Two particularly noteworthy prose speeches include the sermon at the temple, which announces God's freedom to destroy the temple if such action is warranted (chap. 7), and Jeremiah's visit to the potter's house (chap. 18). The symbolic actions include not marrying or participating in community gatherings (chap. 16) and breaking a pot (chap. 19). In the laments (11:18—12:6; 15:10-21; 17:14-18; 18:18-23; 20:7-18), Jeremiah decried the harshness of God's call, the loneliness and brutality of his life, and God's seeming inactivity in fulfilling divine judgment. The narratives about Jeremiah, traditionally attributed to his scribal associate Baruch, are found largely in chaps. 26–29 and 32–44. These chapters contain accounts of Jeremiah's life including: his sermon in the temple (chap. 26), various encounters with leaders (chaps. 27–29), buying property in Anathoth on the eve of the exile (chap. 32), dictating the scroll to Baruch (chap. 36), and his imprisonment and the fall of Judah (chaps. 37–44). Central to the book is a small collection of oracles (chaps. 30–

31), often called the "little book of comfort." Here the LORD promises a new covenant with his people which will be written on the heart. Jeremiah ends with oracles against the nations (chaps. 46–51) and a historical appendix (chap. 52).

Distinctive Features. Readers have frequently noted the numerous ties between Jeremiah and a Deuteronomistic view of the world and history. For example, both stress notions of reward and punishment, obedience to God's law, and the promise of land. These similarities are variously explained as: Deuteronomistic thinking influencing Jeremiah, Jeremiah influencing the Deuteronomists, some later editorial work on the book of Jeremiah, or common attitudes shared during Josiah's reform. In the end, the final perspective of both Jeremiah and the Deuteronomists was the same—both look back from the stark reality of the exile and ask, "Why?"

Most notable in Jeremiah is the presence of personal laments. Through the laments, the private anxiety of the prophet and his struggle and relationship with God become part of the message of the book. Though the prophet is personally rejected, he is vindicated in the end. The laments provide, in part, the model of the suffering servant of Isaiah and eventually the suffering Messiah.

Central Themes. Jeremiah denounces Israel's faithlessness and emphasizes the centrality of devotion and loyalty to the one true God. He denounces dependence on the temple, which he proclaims is not inviolable and provides only false security. He urges repentance, and when such is not forthcoming, he announces the end. The true prophetic word prevails over all attempts, external and internal, to silence the prophet. But Jeremiah also proclaims words of comfort and hope. God's promise of land stands, as does the promise to Jerusalem and the temple, the Davidic dynasty, and the united kingdom. Finally, God promises a new covenant with the people in which forgiveness is followed by everlasting and faithful obedience.

LAMENTATIONS

Date, Author, and Setting. Lamentations, written after the fall of Judah and Jerusalem in 587/586 B.C., is traditionally ascribed to Jeremiah, though his authorship is questionable. The laments, either individually or together, probably formed part of a service of lamentation at the site of the destroyed temple, perhaps on the day of Tabernacles, which was formerly a day of rejoicing (see Zech. 7:1-7; 8:19).

Contents. Lamentations contains five community laments of poignant beauty which bemoan the destruction of Jerusalem. In chapter 1 Jerusalem is portrayed as a lonely widow who has pursued after lovers other than God and is now without comfort. She mourns the loss of her festivals, people, and princes, and she despairs over the victory of her enemies. Chapter 2 laments the LORD's anger and destruction of the city, priesthood, sanctuary, kingship, prophets, and people. Chapter 3, which begins with a description of distress and desolation, moves toward hope in God's love, mercy, and compassion. Chapter 4 returns to a vivid description of death and carnage amidst the destruction of Zion. And chapter 5, in which the community pleads with the LORD to remember his people who are now portrayed as orphans, describes once again the struggles of those left behind. Lamentations ends with an affirmation of faith followed by a plea for restoration and questions about the extent of God's rejection and anger.

Distinctive Features. The first four laments are in the form of acrostics, that is, each of the twenty-two verses begins with a new letter of the Hebrew alphabet. The last lament, though not an acrostic, also has twenty-two verses. The first laments imitate funeral dirges in many respects; chapter 3 is voiced by an individual; and the last chapter is a more formal community lament. The recurrent image of Jerusalem as a woman dominates Lamentations. She mourns her husband's desertion and her children's suffering and death. She reprimands, is reprimanded, seeks comfort, and weeps.

Central Themes. Lamentations is filled with recognizable themes found in the laments of Psalms, Job, and elsewhere including: questions to God, complaints about the victory and gloating of the enemy, acknowledgment of sin, description of hardships, petitions and complaints, recalling the past, and flashes of desperate hope.

Lamentations gives expression to the intense and moving experience of public mourning, of coming to grips with loss. The poet recognizes exile and destruction as punishment by the LORD for sinful transgressions. The power and presence of God is never doubted, and loss is never attributed to the victory of other gods. Lamentations thus provides us with an example of profound faith in the face of tremendous suffering in which mourning, questioning, and even anger are given voice.

EZEKIEL

Identity of Prophet and Date. Ezekiel, the third of the major prophets, overlaps in time with Jeremiah. Ezekiel was a priest exported to Babylon with other community elite ten years before the final exile. According to the dates given in the book, he prophesied in Babylon from 593 until 571 B.C. Little is known about Ezekiel, perhaps the first prophet to deliver all his words in writing, except that he was childless, his wife died just before the fall of Jerusalem, and his behavior frequently borders on the bizarre.

Contents. The book begins with Ezekiel's call (chaps. 1–3), an elaborate vision of the LORD, enthroned above the winged creatures on his chariot. This vision is followed by oracles of judgment that condemn abominations and uncleanness, worship of idols, false prophecy, continual apostasy, and rejection of God's laws (chaps. 4–24). Included are accounts of numerous symbolic actions involving such things as bricks, extended periods of immobility, special meals, and shorn hair. At the center of this section is found a vision of the destruction of the temple and the departure of God's glory (chaps. 8–11). This vision is followed by a series of frequently complex allegories of a vine consumed by fire, an unfaithful wife, an eagle, a cedar, a lioness, and two fallen sisters (chaps. 15–19, 23).

After a series of oracles against the nations (chaps. 25–32) and a summary and transitional chapter (chap. 33), Ezekiel moves gradually to oracles of hope (chaps. 34–48). Highlights include the image of the LORD as good shepherd (chap. 34), a dramatic vision of the valley of dry bones resurrected by the breath and spirit of the LORD (chap. 37), and an apocalyptic vision of Gog and Magog (chaps. 38–39). These last oracles are dominated by a final vision of a new temple (chaps. 40–48) to which the divine glory has returned and by renewed ordinances and a sacred river, lined by healing trees, flowing from the temple through Jerusalem on to refresh the Dead Sea.

Distinctive Features. The language of Ezekiel is unique among the prophets. The book is composed largely of lengthy, elaborate, frequently obscure and repetitive prose accounts which are richly and sometimes repugnantly detailed. The first-person style presents the prophet, addressed regularly as "mortal" (Hebrew: "son of man") as receiving and delivering his prophetic words directly from God.

Central Themes. Ezekiel places tremendous emphasis on recognition of the holy, just, and omnipotent LORD. The continual stress on God's glory projects a somewhat distant, always transcendent and mysterious God. Ezekiel emphasizes as well the importance of individual responsibility (chaps. 14, 18, 33) whereby people are saved by their righteousness or condemned by their wickedness. The book moves steadily from condemnation to hope. The condemnation stands as a warning that is not negated by the hope. The hope is tied to the visions of the future in which united Israel will be restored with a new heart and a new spirit, creation will be renewed, and all Israel will gather to the LORD's temple.

DANIEL

Date, Author, and Purpose. The book of Daniel is included as the final book in the major prophets in the Christian canon. Though set in Babylon over a seventy-year period (606–536 B.C.) that includes the exile, Daniel actually dates from around 167–164 during the Jewish persecution by the Greek king, Antiochus IV Epiphanes (175–163). The author was probably a pious Jew living in Jerusalem writing to inspire the faithful among his contemporaries and to give them hope.

Contents. This book of Daniel is composed of six narratives (chaps. 1–6) and four dream-visions (chaps. 7–12). In most of the narratives, Daniel, the hero of the book, stands over against either Babylonian kings Nebuchadnezzar (chaps. 1–4) and Belshazzar (chap. 5) or the Persian king Darius (chap. 6) and their advisors. Daniel is pictured as a pious, righteous, and wise high-ranking member of the court who is able through faith: to accomplish miraculous feats, such as surviving the lion's den; to reveal dreams to the king; to offer true interpretations of these dreams; to read mysterious handwriting on the wall; and, above all, to bring the king to recognize the true God, the God of the Jews. Daniel's piety is shown through his refusing the king's unclean food, through his prayers, and through his wisdom, by which he earns recognition, stature, and honor. Chapter 3 tells an independent narrative about three Jewish youth, Shadrach, Meshach, and Abednego, who, after refusing to worship an image King Nebuchadnezzar sets up, are thrown into a fiery furnace and are miraculously delivered.

The dreams and visions of Daniel found in chapters 7–12 include images of four great beasts, the throne of the "Ancient One," the appearance of "one like a human being" (chap. 7), a ram and goat (chap. 8), a prayer of confession and supplication by Daniel and an interpretation of the seventy years (chap. 9), and an angelic call (chap. 10), which introduces a great apocalyptic vision of the last days of history inscribed in the book of truth (chaps. 11–12).

Distinctive Features. Daniel represents the beginning of the kind of apocalyptic writing that is futuristic, looking toward the final days. This writing grows out of both the wisdom and prophetic traditions and culminates in the New Testament book of Revelation. As apocalyptic writing, Daniel communicates on a cosmic and universal scale through symbols and signs, end times, and cosmic secrets. Daniel is filled with dreams, visions, interpretations, angels with specific names, battles, and multiple images of hybrid beasts and other intricately detailed figures.

Central Themes. The book of Daniel shows forth the power, justice, and trustworthiness of the "Most High" God of the Jews. The LORD resides in heaven, rules over all the earth, over all time, and over all people. Therefore all people should repent and worship this God alone. Interpretations and visions of history show those who currently hold earthly power will not in the end be victorious. They can and will be replaced by the pious saints, the lowly but faithful, who will receive everlasting life. Just as Babylon and Persia were defeated, so also will the current tyrants from Greece be eliminated through the victory of cosmic forces. The ultimate judgment will come from heaven in the later days when persecution will come to an end, good will prevail over evil, and all will be revealed.

■

The final twelve books of the Old Testament together make up the minor prophets, or the "Book of the Twelve." This collection of shorter prophetic books seems to have been a unit by early in the second century B.C. Each book begins, as did Isaiah and Jeremiah, with a formal superscription announcing the "word," "vision," or "oracle" of the LORD or the prophet and gives some

small piece of biographical information. Many of the books move from announcements of doom to announcements of hope, a movement felt to a degree in the whole collection. The collection moves roughly, though not strictly, from earlier to later prophets. However, Hosea, not Amos, comes first, perhaps because of his intimate and ultimately hopeful vision, and the collection ends with Malachi's forward-looking proclamation of the coming of Elijah in the day of judgment.

HOSEA

Identity of Prophet and Date. Hosea is the only prophet from the Northern Kingdom of Israel among the major and minor prophets. His prophetic career began in the last years of the prosperous reign of Jeroboam II (786–746) and continued through the disintegration of the kingdom until its ultimate fall to the Assyrians in 722/721.

Contents. The first three chapters of Hosea recount, in some detail, Hosea's marriage to Gomer, who is committed to a life of harlotry, and the birth of her three children, who are given the symbolic names of Jezreel (God sows), Lo-ruhamah (not pitied), and Lo-ammi (not my people). Hosea's marriage is described, not out of biographical interest in the prophet, but because Hosea's reaction to Gomer's infidelity provides the central metaphor for God's relationship to Israel: God remains faithful even in the face of Israel's promiscuous involvement with other gods. God's faithfulness ultimately transforms "not pities" into "pitied" and "not my people" into "you are my people." In chapters 4–11, Hosea announces judgment against Israel for numerous acts of unfaithfulness, including: breaking the covenant, deceptive priests and prophets, false princes and nobles, Baalism and false worship, cult prostitution, injustice, and faithless dependence on alliances with Egypt and Babylon. This section ends with a moving metaphor in which Israel is the rebellious son, unable to respond appropriately to parental love, and God is the loving parent whose unending compassion cannot allow judgment to prevail. The final three chapters repeat the movement from judgment to compassion by rehearsing again Israel's past iniquities and announcing God's ultimate mercy.

Distinctive Features. Hosea continually makes use of luxuriant and forceful language that is often difficult to unravel or even to translate. The book is filled with metaphorical imagery: God is portrayed as husband, father, mother, shepherd, pus, decay, lion, bear, physician, baker, fowler, farmer, vinedresser, dew, and evergreen cypress who offers fruit. Israel, for its part, is pictured as unfaithful wife, heifer, lamb, sickness, infected sore, dew, spoiled cake, silly dove, vine, rebellious son, morning mist, and lily. The fluidity of movement from one image and subject to the next makes it difficult to separate the words of Hosea into individual units of speech, but moves the book unrelentingly forward.

Central Themes. Hosea offers strong condemnation of Israel matched by equally intense hope. The prophet calls on Israel to return to the LORD, to abandon apostasy, to live a life based on fidelity and commitment, and to "know" the LORD. If such knowledge should prevail, all else would follow. At the core of Hosea stands the dynamic tension between God's righteous judgment on one hand, and on the other, the divine pathos of God's loyal and unending love.

JOEL

Identity of Prophet and Date. The superscription, different from most of the prophetic books, does not designate any historic time period for Joel. Given the prophet's use of previous prophetic material and his reference both to the exile and the rebuilt temple, most scholars place Joel, perhaps a "cultic prophet" (associated with the temple), in Jerusalem near the end of the Persian period (538–333 A.D.).

Contents. Joel begins by calling on the community to listen to what has happened and to pass the news on to future generations. He then proceeds to describe in detail a terrible plague of locusts (1:4—2:11). He makes use of the image of the "day of the LORD," which was once looked upon as a day to be welcomed when the LORD would defeat Israel's enemies, but now the day is dreaded. Interspersed with this description, Joel laments, cries to the LORD, and calls on others to join him in lamentation, fasting, and repentance. The LORD, in turn, hears the prayer of the people, has pity, and promises the end of the plague and the restoration of the fortunes of Judah and Jerusalem (2:18-27). The LORD then announces a future "day of the LORD" in which God will pour out the spirit of prophecy on all the people of later generations, will fight against the nations, will seek revenge for the wrongs done to Judah, and will take up residence once more in Zion.

Distinctive Features. The book of Joel has frequently been identified as a cultic, prophetic liturgy because of: numerous expressions in familiar set patterns (for example, 2:12-14); frequent references to the temple and its services; the use of the "day of the LORD"; the repeated calls to proclamation, lamentation, and repentance; and an overall movement from lamentation to pronouncement.

Central Themes. Joel takes a natural disaster, a plague of locusts, and transforms it into a cosmic and apocalyptic "day of the LORD." Joel then uses the disaster and its aftermath as a timeless warning to the people to repent and put their hope in the LORD. Through the words of the LORD that Joel proclaims, the people know that the LORD is in their midst and will dwell in Zion forever.

AMOS

Identity of Prophet and Date. Amos is the earliest of the prophets included in the prophetic books. His prophecies, which date from the reign of Jeroboam II (786–746 B.C.), overlap with those of Hosea, though Amos begins and ends somewhat earlier. Amos, like Hosea, speaks to the Northern Kingdom of Israel, though Amos himself comes from Tekoa, a small town in the Southern Kingdom of Judah. Amos was not a professional prophet; rather he was called from the care of flocks and sycamore trees in Judah to proclaim God's word of judgment to Israel.

Contents. The book of Amos begins with a series of judgment oracles—first against the nations that surround Israel, including Judah, and eventually against Israel herself (chaps. 1–2). Israel is condemned specifically for the lack of social justice, trampling upon the poor and needy, and attempting to silence the prophetic word. Amos proclaims before the nations that Israel will be judged for her oppression and violence so that only a small remnant will remain. He gives a series of divine words (chaps. 3–4), a series of woe-oracles (5:18—6:8), and has a series of visions (chaps. 7–9), all aimed at revealing Israel's injustice in the market, the temple, the judicial court, and in all aspects of daily life. Chapter 7 reports a crucial encounter between Amos and Amaziah, a priest of Bethel, the king's sanctuary. Amaziah accuses Amos of conspiracy against the king and attempts to send him away, but Amos responds that his call and words are from the LORD, and renews his prophecy of judgment. The book ends with two oracles of future salvation (9:11-15).

Distinctive Features. Amos is particularly noted for his ironic use of reversal: Israel thinks other nations will be judged, but Israel will be judged; the day of the LORD will be darkness, not light; the "first" among the rich will be the "first" to go into exile, and so forth. His language, which uses few metaphors except that of the LORD roaring like a lion, is direct and uncompromising.

Central Themes. Israel tries to silence God's word delivered by the prophet, but ends with harsher words of judgment, or worse, a deafening silence that signals God's judgment all the louder. Amos proclaims that social injustice and abuse of the poor constitute a profanation of God's holy name. The people of Israel believe they are protected by worship, by God's promise, and by being God's chosen people, but Amos announces that precisely *because* Israel is special, the people are to be held accountable for their actions. Of all the prophets Amos is clearest in his proclamation that the LORD cares passionately that "justice roll down like waters, and righteousness like an everflowing stream" (5:24).

OBADIAH

Identity of Prophet and Date. Obadiah is difficult to date. The opening oracle may have been delivered shortly after the defeat of Judah by Babylon, when Edom sided against Judah (587/586 B.C.). In the light of Edom's own subsequent defeat, the book was later expanded during the postexilic period (600–400). Nothing is known of the prophet, whose common name *Obadiah* means "servant of the LORD."

Contents. Obadiah, the shortest book in the Old Testament, has only one chapter. Obadiah begins with an oracle against Edom, the nation descended from Esau that was a traditional enemy of Judah. Obadiah condemns Edom for "the slaughter and violence done to your brother Jacob" and for rejoicing in and contributing to Judah's misfortune. He then announces the coming of the day of the LORD in which Edom and other nations will be judged, and Mount Zion and the house of Jacob will be restored.

Central Themes. The book of Obadiah, whose beginning oracle bears marked resemblance to the oracle against Edom found in Jeremiah 49:7-16, uses the fate of one nation, Edom, to reflect on the LORD's general judgment of the nations. The exile does not have the last word; the people of Israel and Judah shall possess the land of their enemies, and "the kingdom shall be the LORD's."

JONAH

Identity of Prophet and Date. The book of Jonah, unlike the other prophetic books, is an independent narrative *about* a prophet rather than a collection of prophetic words. The book, which ostensibly takes place during the reign of Jeroboam II (786–746 B.C.), centers on the figure of Jonah, a prophet mentioned briefly in 2 Kings 14:25. Scholars have suggested various dates for the writing of the book ranging from preexilic to late postexilic times. Given the possible influence of earlier books and the theme of relationship to foreign nations, a postexilic date around 500-400 is most probable.

Contents. The narrative begins with a word of the LORD instructing Jonah to go to Nineveh, the principal city of Assyria, Israel's major foe. Jonah was to warn Nineveh that God was aware of the great wickedness in that city. But Jonah, instead of responding to this call, fled in the opposite direction and boarded a ship to Tarshish, probably located in what is now southern Spain. The LORD then sent a mighty storm which caused the sailors aboard to seek divine guidance. When they found that Jonah was fleeing the LORD, they reluctantly threw him overboard and besought the LORD's forgiveness and favor. The LORD then sent a great fish that saved Jonah from drowning in the chaotic seas and delivered him, after a prayer of thanksgiving (chap. 2), upon the dry land. Chapter 3 begins with a second call to Jonah to go to the despised city of Nineveh. This time Jonah did as he was asked and briefly delivered God's oracle of destruction. Immediately the people of Nineveh believed in God and repented of their wicked ways. God responded by calling off the destruction of the city. In chapter 4 Jonah expressed his anger at God's mercy towards Nineveh and begged to die. God instead sent a plant that afforded temporary shade to Jonah and then caused the plant to die, which brought distress to Jonah. God then told Jonah that Nineveh, with all its people and cattle, deserved Jonah's compassion more than the plant.

Distinctive Features. The book of Jonah, like so many of the narratives in the Old Testament, was written with consummate skill, with humor, and with great attention to detail. The author of Jonah had a tremendous sense of irony. The foreigners, both the sailors and the people of Nineveh, had more faith in and understanding of the LORD, the God of Israel, than did Jonah, God's chosen prophet.

Central Themes. The book of Jonah explores issues of the nature of prophecy, the problems of nationalism, and the freedom of God. The book explores the meaning of the traditional description of God as "a gracious God and merciful, slow to anger, and abounding in steadfast love, and ready to relent from punishing" (4:2). Jonah represents a nationalistic prophet with a narrow view of God's judgment and grace. He believed that the LORD would protect and care for him and the people Israel by virtue of their being chosen. Instead God is shown to have the freedom to judge or to have mercy upon whomever God chooses. God is open to withhold mercy from Jonah, and more significantly, to attend to the repentant prayers of foreigners and to grant to them forgiveness and salvation.

MICAH

Identity of Prophet and Date. Micah spoke to the Southern Kingdom of Judah through the period of the collapse of the North (742–698 B.C.), starting after but overlapping with Isaiah. Little is known of Micah except that he came from the small Judean town of Moresheth, southwest of Jerusalem. The core of the book was perhaps expanded several times by various generations of disciples.

Contents. As in Hosea, the book of Micah contains a thrice repeated pattern of oracles of doom followed by oracles of hope. In chapters 1–2 Micah speaks as a Southerner but disdains the opulence of both Samaria, the capital city of Israel, and Jerusalem, the capital of the Southern Kingdom of Judah. The wickedness of the North has infected the South with idolatry, injustice, and oppression. Still, a remnant will be saved with "the Lord at their head" (2:12-13). In chapter 3 Micah repeats a call for justice and cries against false prophets and all corrupt leaders who give deceptive assurances of peace. Yet in the latter days: all nations will flow to Jerusalem to learn the law; swords will be converted into plowshares; the remnant of Judah will be restored; little Bethlehem will give birth to a future king; the enemies will be defeated; and idolatry will cease (chaps. 4–5). In the third cycle of oracles Micah describes Judah's unjust response to God's history of redemption and announces yet again the coming judgment of Judah's apostasy, false worship, and wickedness in all levels of family and society (6:1—7:7). Micah ends with what seems a liturgical call to hope (7:8-20), in which hymnic praises assure the people that God's judgment will give way to light, God's anger will become compassion, and God's faithfulness to and love for Jacob will prevail.

Distinctive Features. Micah's message most closely resembles the earlier oracles of Isaiah, a prophet with whom he has strong literary ties. However, unlike Isaiah, Micah looks for and predicts the fall of Jerusalem. Micah's rich use of language is reflected both in his promises, particularly in chapters 4–5, and in his demands: "what does the LORD require of you but to do justice, and to love kindness, and to walk humbly with your God?" (6:8).

Central Themes. Like his contemporaries, Isaiah, Amos, and Hosea, Micah spoke out against injustice and announced the need to turn away from wickedness and false worship. Micah was remembered by the people of Jeremiah's day as one whose words of warning caused King Hezekiah to repent (Jer. 26:18-19). But Micah was remembered most among the writers of the New Testament for his vision of a future messianic king who will feed his flock "in the strength of the LORD" (5:4).

NAHUM

Identity of Prophet, Historical Setting, and Date. Nahum, together with Jeremiah, Habakkuk, and Zephaniah, prophesied during the last half-century of the kingdom of Judah, which fell to the Babylonians in 587/586 B.C. Nahum, whose name means "comfort," announced to the people of Judah, sometime around 620, the coming downfall of the city of Nineveh, the capital of Assyria. The Assyrians, who had destroyed the Northern Kingdom of Israel a century before and had come near to destroying Judah as well, were the overlords of Judah until the Assyrians were defeated by the Medes and Babylonians beginning around 630. Nineveh fell in 612.

Contents. The book of Nahum, made up of three short chapters, contains a classic prophetic oracle against a foreign nation. Nahum opens with a vivid poetic description of the avenging power and determination of the LORD. Chapter 1 moves then to a proclamation that Judah has been avenged and the enemy has been cut off. Chapters 2–3 give a detailed and triumphant description of the destruction of Nineveh by the forces of the LORD of hosts.

Distinctive Features. Nahum begins with an incomplete and altered acrostic poem in which the first eleven verses begin with the first eleven letters of the Hebrew alphabet. The use of this device, combined with the stylized language of holy war and the skillful use of poetic movement, suggests that the book may have been used liturgically.

Central Theme. Nahum's message is direct and specific. The LORD is a just and jealous God who will not ignore an evil nation nor leave the destruction of his people unavenged. Nineveh has wrought destruction, served idols, and betrayed nations; therefore Nineveh will be destroyed. Let all people rejoice, "For who has ever escaped your [Assyria's] endless cruelty?" (3:19).

HABAKKUK

Identity of Prophet and Date. Habakkuk prophesied to Judah just after Nahum, probably during the reign of Jehoiakim (609–598 B.C.), during which time Judah became a vassal state to the Babylonians. Little is known about Habakkuk, but, given his use of personal laments and hymns, he was perhaps a prophetic leader associated with the temple.

Contents. Habakkuk, like Nahum, contains three chapters, but in this case the book has three distinctive parts: First, chapters 1:2—2:5 contain a twofold conversation between the prophet and God. Habakkuk begins with a lament bemoaning destruction, violence, and the lack of punishment for the wicked; God responds that he is rousing the Babylonians to bring justice and to destroy the guilty (1:2-11). Habakkuk then offers a second lament complaining about the faithlessness of the Babylonians and questioning God's apparently unjust treatment of the wicked and the righteous. God responds with a command that Habakkuk write a vision upon tablets, declaring that although the unrighteous will fail, "the righteous live by their faith" (2:4). Second, the five woe-oracles that follow condemn dishonest plunderers set on their own gain, those who corrupt others and commit violence, and those who worship idols. Assurance is given that the wicked ultimately will be punished, for "the LORD is in his holy temple" (2:6-20). Third, chapter 3 contains a dramatic and powerful hymn which describes the coming of the LORD in magnificent, cosmic terms. The book ends with a commitment to rejoice in the LORD, God of salvation and strength.

Distinctive Features. Habakkuk contains powerful language that mixes national and individual concerns about how God is working out the divine promises and how justice is finally served. Though the book may well have been edited over time, the single-minded drive toward faith in a just and righteous God is relentless and compelling.

Central Themes. Several significant questions stand behind Habakkuk's words. Why do the wicked go unpunished while the righteous suffer? Why are the Babylonians allowed to defeat God's people? How shall the righteous respond? What will be the end? Will God's promises and justice prevail? God continually responds that his ways, though mysterious, are just. God can both use

Babylon as avenger and later judge Babylon for its sins. The righteous shall, like Habakkuk himself, live by faith and trust in the LORD. In the end, God's justice will prevail, for "the earth will be filled with the knowledge of the glory of the LORD, as the waters cover the sea" (2:14).

ZEPHANIAH

Identity of Prophet and Date. Zephaniah spoke during the reign of Josiah (640–609 B.C.), who ruled during the short period of time between foreign overlords. In this period Josiah's deuteronomistic reforms first took hold and then failed. Zephaniah was perhaps one of the prophets who, like Jeremiah, helped initiate the reforms and then bemoaned their failure.

Contents. The book of Zephaniah, like the two previous books, contains three chapters. In chapter 1, which contains words of judgment against Judah and Jerusalem for idol worship, apostasy, disloyalty, and unbelief, Zephaniah announces the coming day of the LORD against the whole earth and its inhabitants. In chapter 2 Zephaniah turns his prediction of the day of the LORD against the surrounding nations and specifically against the mighty Assyria. Only those who seek the LORD, those "humble of the land who do God's commandments," will perhaps escape God's wrath (v. 3). In chapter 3, Zephaniah begins by renewing the announcement of judgment against Jerusalem and the nations (vv. 1-7), but moves quickly to an oracle of salvation that announces a time when all peoples and all nations will call on the name of the LORD (vv. 8-13). The book ends with an exultant hymn celebrating the end of judgment against Jerusalem followed by renewed salvation oracles in which the lame and the outcast are gathered together and Zion's fortunes are restored before the nations (vv. 14-20).

Central Themes. Zephaniah skillfully combines sweeping and cosmic words of judgment with dramatic and all-encompassing words of hope. He particularly disdains lack of humility

71

and lack of faith in the ultimate power and justice of the LORD. The day of the LORD will come against both Judah and the nations, but the restoration will include both as well. Zephaniah envisions a time in which the LORD will rule over Jerusalem in love, and the haughty shall be replaced by those who seek refuge in the LORD; "then they will pasture and lie down, and no one shall make them afraid" (3:13).

HAGGAI

Identity of Prophet and Date. The final three minor prophets, Haggai, Zechariah, and Malachi, join Third Isaiah as the leading prophetic voices of Jerusalem's tiny and struggling postexilic community. Haggai is dated specifically during the second year of the Persian king Darius I (521–485 B.C.). Haggai prophesied in Jerusalem in 520 when Zerubbabel, a descendant of David, was governor and Joshua, a Zadokite, was high priest. In Ezra 5:1 and 6:14 Haggai is commended, along with Zechariah, for his prophetic role in the rebuilding of the temple in Jerusalem.

Contents. In chapter 1 Haggai delivers an oracle of the LORD to the people of postexilic Judah, explaining that the reason that the people were suffering economic hardship was their failure to rebuild the house of the LORD. Under the leadership of Zerubbabel and Joshua, the people responded to Haggai and began to rebuild the temple. According to chapter 2, Haggai received three more oracles during the next five months. In the first oracle he exhorted the people to take courage, for the LORD would shake the heavens and the earth to collect the material necessary to make the second temple more glorious than the first. In the second oracle Haggai warned against contamination by an unclean people, perhaps the Samaritans. In the final oracle Haggai proclaimed that the nations would be overthrown, and Zerubbabel, the new Davidic king, would lead in the messianic age.

Distinctive Features. The book of Haggai, like much of the final two prophetic books, is written in prose rather than poetry.

Haggai's style is reminiscent of the writing found in the historical books.

Central Themes. The message of Haggai is single-minded and direct. The people of Judah were to rebuild the temple. This rebuilding would provide blessing for the struggling postexilic community, which had little external reason for hope. Haggai insisted that God's promises were still to be fulfilled: the LORD would be honored (1:8), and a Davidic king would reign once more (2:23).

ZECHARIAH

Identity of Prophet and Date. Zechariah, like Haggai, was active during the early postexilic period and is mentioned in Ezra for his prophetic words about rebuilding the temple. The first eight chapters of the book were delivered by Zechariah in Jerusalem between 520 and 518 B.C. The final five chapters, sometimes designated Second Zechariah, come from anonymous writers from a later period between 500 and 400.

Contents. The first eight chapters of Zechariah are dominated by a series of eight visions: (1) of myrtle trees and angels who bring comfort to Zion and promise a rebuilt temple; (2) of horns of the nations who will be scattered; (3) of a vastly expanded Jerusalem with the LORD dwelling in her midst; (4) of Joshua, the Zadokite high priest, and Satan standing before the LORD, in which Satan is rebuked and a richly clothed Joshua receives the promise of a new Davidic branch; (5) of a golden lampstand beside two olive trees; (6) of a flying scroll condemning those who steal and swear falsely; (7) of a woman signifying sin; and (8) of four chariots with horses that go forth to patrol all the corners of the earth. These visions are framed by oracular materials (chap. 1:1-17; chaps. 7–8) that review and summarize the history of the prophetic word to the people. These oracles explain how the people had been told to repent of their evil ways and to show kindness and mercy. The people had refused to listen and had been scattered among the nations. Now the LORD has returned to gather the remnant of the people to himself, to turn lamentation and fasting into "seasons of joy and gladness" (8:19), and to cause the nations to seek the LORD in Jerusalem and to entreat his favor.

The final chapters of Zechariah contain a series of oracles that begin with the downfall of the nations and the triumphant return of Israel's king. Both Israel and Judah will be restored but also judged. Zechariah uses the image of the shepherd to reflect on the history of foreign rule and Israelite apostasy (chap. 11). In chapters 12–14 Zechariah describes the final victory of the LORD, in which the house of David leads a triumphant defeat of the nations, Jerusalem is purged of idolatry and false prophecy, the shepherd dies for his sheep, the covenant is renewed, and a great cosmic battle takes place that transforms the world—banning cold, frost, and night, creating living waters, and causing all nations to come to Jerusalem to worship the king.

Distinctive Features. The eight visions found in the first chapters of Zechariah are reported in familiar set patterns and then interpreted by angels. The oracles in these chapters lift up the message of the classical prophets and call on the people to repent. The final chapters, whose vocabulary, style, and content differ considerably from chapters 1–8, introduce apocalyptic elements dealing with battles and the image of triumphant Jerusalem.

Central Themes. Zechariah looks on all activity from a cosmic perspective. Something new is happening. Significant connections are made between heaven and earth and between Jerusalem and the nations. The book presses forward to the LORD's future victory. In the first part of the book, emphasis is placed on the centrality of Jerusalem, the future of the Davidic king and the Zadokite priesthood, and the repentance of the people. The second part of Zechariah concentrates on the end times when the nations are destroyed while Israel is restored. The future is marked by intense struggle and judgment. Zechariah is noted especially for his messianic pictures that point forward to the New Testament: the image of the king who ". . . comes to you . . . humble and riding on a donkey . . ." (9:9); false shepherds paying the king a slave's wage of thirty shekels of silver (11:13); and the image of the Davidic king, pierced by others yet full of a spirit of compassion and supplication (12:10).

MALACHI

Identity of Prophet and Date. The final prophetic book is Malachi, a word that means simply "my messenger" and was probably not intended as a name. This anonymous prophecy was delivered during the reign of Xerxes I (486–465) after the restoration of the temple and just prior to the governorship of Nehemiah.

Contents. The book of Malachi forms basically one unit in which the LORD responds to some questions from the people and then asks some questions of his own. In chapter 1 Malachi is concerned about the nature of God's love, the honor given by the priests to the LORD, and the purity of sacrifice. This concern continues in chapter 2, in which the Zadokite priests are rebuked for corrupting the "covenant with Levi" and failing to lead the people in the way of the law. Malachi speaks out against faithlessness in both divine and marriage covenants. He exhorts people to believe in the God of justice. Chapter 3 opens with an announcement that the LORD is sending his messenger to prepare the way and asks "who can endure the day of his coming?" (3:2). He speaks of the coming judgment as like "a refiner's fire," purifying the sons of Levi, and as a swift witness against sorcerers, adulterers, liars, oppressors, and those who do not fear the LORD. Malachi calls for true repentance and speaks of the LORD's recognition of the righteous. The final chapter, chapter 4: announces the coming of the day of the LORD in which the wicked will burn and the righteous will be healed; calls on Israel to remember the law of Moses; and announces the return of Elijah the prophet who will call for repentance before that "great and terrible day" (4:5).

Distinctive Features. Malachi contains a series of extended disputations, often introduced by questions alternating between God and the people in general or the priests in particular. God's answers to these questions emphasize covenant, law, and the justice of God and give both exhortation and judgment.

Central Themes. Malachi in many ways returns to the dramatic call for repentance found in the preexilic prophets. He calls on the priests and on all of the people to heed the law, to seek justice and obedience, and to worship the LORD in purity and holiness. He proclaims both the love of God for his people and the judgment of God that will not compromise with wickedness. The Old Testament thus ends on a note of warning rather than hope. Repent, for the day of the LORD draws near! The predicted coming of Elijah to repeat this warning sounds an alarm picked up in the Gospel accounts of John the Baptist, and this alarm rings on in the ears of generations of believers struggling to remain faithful.

Part 2

The New Testament

Reading the New Testament is much like touring an unknown region of the world for the first time. The landscape is breathtaking, the culture intriguing, and the people fascinating. But what makes this tour so exciting is how quickly and readily you start to identify the familiar within the unfamiliar. The intriguing new culture begins to look amazingly like your own! As you come to know the fascinating people, they gradually seem more and more like you. And the landscape! It is dominated by a single outstanding figure: Jesus of Nazareth, and his life, death, and resurrection.

The New Testament is something of a foreign land to many. But with a guided tour through the New Testament writings, their stories and their authors, the once foreign land becomes as personal as home itself. In this world of the New Testament everything pivots around the Christ figure. Each of the authors attempts in his or her own way to explore the meaning of Christ for human life. Everything arises from the faith that God has done something novel and beneficial in the prophet from Galilee some two thousand years ago. But what does it all mean for daily life? That is the single, persistent subject of the New Testament. You are invited now on a tour into that world to discover its beauty and meaning for yourself.

The books of the New Testament are of five types. The first type is *Gospel* and includes the books called Matthew, Mark, Luke, and John. The Acts of the Apostles stands alone in representing a kind of *historical narrative.* The largest number of books are classified as *epistles or letters,* specifically, Romans, 1 and 2 Corinthians, Galatians, Ephesians, Philippians, Colossians, 1 and 2 Thessalonians, 1 and 2 Timothy, Titus, Philemon, 1 and 2 Peter, 2 and 3 John, and Jude. *Tracts or sermons* are represented in Hebrews, James, and 1 John. Revelation is alone in a category labeled *apocalypse.*

The Gospels tell the story of Jesus of Nazareth and thereby proclaim the good news of what God has done for humanity through him. The Acts of the Apostles relates the story of the spread of Christianity throughout the Roman Empire. The epistles are examples of the correspondence among Christians in the first century of the Christian era. Sometimes they are addressed to a whole congregation (for example, Romans) and sometimes to individual Christians within a congregation (see Philemon). In either case, they include elements common to letters in the Roman world of the time: The author's and recipient's names, a greeting and thanksgiving, the body of the letter, and a conclusion that usually includes a wish for peace, and a grace (or benediction).

The sermons or tracts are often like letters but lack some of the major features usually found in ancient correspondence. They are written on particular subjects and were intended for circulation among a number of Christian churches. It is not always clear whether they were developed from oral presentations to one congregation into a more general message for a wider audience, or whether they were originally written for general reading.

The apocalypse relates an author's visionary experience having to do with God's future acts. Typical of apocalyptic writing, the message is couched in elaborate symbolism and through the symbols encourages the reader to faithfulness in the face of hardship.

The Gospels

The four Gospels—Matthew, Mark, Luke, and John—introduce the dominant figure in the landscape of the New Testament. They all share the common feature of narrating the ministry of Jesus of Nazareth with the purpose of describing the importance of Jesus for human life. They are not biographies but use historical information to nurture a faith response to the Christian message about Christ.

The order of the Gospels in our New Testament reflects the fact that the first three are similar, while John is distinct from them. Matthew, Mark, and Luke follow a similar outline in their narratives that is not found in John. The structure of that outline is threefold: Jesus' ministry in Galilee, his journey to Judea, and his ministry, death, and resurrection in Jerusalem. Because of this common pattern, the Gospels of Matthew, Mark, and Luke are called *synoptics*, from Greek words which mean to share a common point of view. The similarities among the synoptics are due, scholars most often argue, to the fact that Mark was the first of the Gospels to be written and was used as a source for the writing of both Matthew and Luke. Those two each used another source that scholars believe was a collection of sayings attributed to Jesus. In addition, Matthew and Luke each had access to different sources uniquely their own. This theory of the sources used by the authors explains why the synoptics all follow a comparable outline in their narratives (that is, the outline of Mark), yet Matthew and Luke share sayings and acts of Jesus not found in Mark. It also suggests the reason why both Matthew and Luke have stories and sayings found only in their respective writings.

The Gospel according to John presents an outline quite different from the synoptics. Jesus is represented as making a number of trips from Galilee to Jerusalem and having a more lengthy ministry in the area of Jerusalem. Moreover, the Gospel of John has an abundance of narratives and discourses of Jesus that are not found in the synoptics. Still, there are parts of John that are comparable to the synoptics. The uniqueness of the fourth Gospel, on the one hand, and its similarities with the synoptics, on the other hand, pose an unsolvable problem. Some believe the author of John knew the synoptics but chose for the most part to write independently of them. Others think that this author did not know the synoptics and wrote without dependence on them. If the latter is the case, some of the sources employed by the fourth evangelist may have contained material similar to the synoptics, thus accounting for both the similarities to and the differences from the synoptics.

MATTHEW

Authorship. Matthew stands first in the New Testament due to its early popularity in the church. The author nowhere gives the reader his name, but tradition has attached the name Matthew. The connection between a Matthew and the author of this Gospel was intended to identify the evangelist with Jesus' disciple, Matthew, the tax collector (10:3 and 9:9; compare the latter with Mark 2:14). Verifying this identification is beyond the range of our knowledge, and the author remains anonymous.

Contents. Matthew has three main parts. In the first part Jesus is presented as the Messiah and Son of God (1:1—4:11) by means of Jesus' genealogy, a narration of his wondrous birth, and the visit of the wise men from the East (1:1—2:23). The preaching of John the Baptist, the baptism of Jesus, and his temptation constitute the remainder of the section (3:1—4:11).

The focus of the second part is on the ministry of Jesus in Galilee, as well as the surrounding territory, and his rejection (4:12—16:20). That ministry is described as teaching, preaching, and healing (4:17—11:1). Within the early portion of this section are an account of the calling of disciples (4:18-22), general statements regarding the beginning of Jesus' ministry (4:17, 23-25), and a collection of his teachings commonly known as the "sermon

on the mount" (5:1—7:29). The sermon is followed by Jesus'
remarkable acts of healing people (see 8:5-13) and affecting nature
(for example, the stilling of the storm, 8:23-27), as well as the
extension of his ministry through the mission of the twelve disciples (10:1-42). The latter half of the second section is devoted
to the rejection of Jesus by the religious leaders (11:2—16:20).
His conflict with the religious leaders is told in such incidents as
Jesus' healing on the sabbath (12:9-14) and his rejection of religious tradition (15:1-20). Recorded here too are the feeding of
the crowds (14:13-21 and 15:32-39), a series of parables (13:1-
52), and Jesus' walking on the sea (14:22-33). The section concludes with Peter's confession of Jesus as the Christ (16:13-20).

The final part of Matthew narrates Jesus' journey to Jerusalem
followed by his suffering, death, and resurrection (16:21—28:20).
The transfiguration of Jesus is told in 17:1-13, teachings about
greatness reported (18:1-14 and 20:20-28), and a number of parables recounted (see 18:23-35 and 20:1-16). The ministry in Jerusalem and the surrounding area is laced with conflict between
Jesus and the religious authorities, including the entry into Jerusalem and the driving of the money changers from the temple
area (21:1-13). Challenges to his authority posed by the leaders
(21:23-46) and his harsh words against them (23:1-39) lead to his
preparation for death (26:1-15). The story of Jesus' last night with
his disciples, the prayer in Gethsemane, arrest, trial, crucifixion,
and resurrection conclude the Gospel (26:17—28:20). The final
scene of the book commissions the disciples for their ministry
(often called "the great commission") and assures the readers of
Christ's continued presence with them (28:16-20).

Distinctive Features. When one thinks of the Gospel of Matthew, most often it is the famous sermon on the mount (5:2—
7:29) that comes to mind. This well-known passage is a collection
of the teachings of Jesus that comprises a kind of "textbook for
discipleship." It is grounded in the radical grace of God suggested
by the beatitudes (5:3-12). Beyond that the sermon describes the
demands of discipleship (for example, 5:20), the character of the

disciple as a person of radical trust in God (for example, 6:25-33), and the role and responsibility of discipleship (5:13-16).

The sermon on the mount exemplifies a number of the unique features of this Gospel, especially in its attention to Jesus' teachings. Among the four Gospels, Matthew has the largest selection of Jesus' instructions regarding morality and Christian discipleship. Within the sermon on the mount stands Matthew's emphasis on the righteousness that characterizes Christian life. Matthew's image of Jesus is that of the Messiah and teacher of God's righteousness and Son of God, whose coming is the realization of God's ancient promise to Israel. Matthew is distinctive in its frequent citation of passages from the Old Testament as evidence of Jesus' fulfillment of prophecy (see, for example, 1:22-23). This is the only Gospel that is explicit in its interest in the church (for example, 18:15-20) and portrays the church as the new and righteous people of God.

Date and Purpose. Matthew was probably written A.D. 80–85 of the Christian era. Its purpose was to present Jesus as the Messiah and the Son of God—"God with us" (1:23). It also sought to sharpen the identity of the Christian church, particularly in relation to Judaism from which the church was separated by the time of the writing of Matthew. Toward that end this Gospel stresses the authority of Jesus' teachings for Christian life (for example, 28:18-20).

MARK

Authorship. The shortest of the Gospels was written by an unnamed Christian leader, first identified as Mark by a second-century bishop. Probably the name was meant to be associated with the John Mark of Acts (see Acts 12:12). Sometimes the mysterious "young man" in 14:51 is taken to be a veiled reference to the author, but such an interpretation is speculative. Equally uncertain is the suggestion that this Gospel represents the recollections of Simon Peter dictated to a secretary in the months preceding his martyrdom. We shall probably never know the identity of the author of this Gospel.

Contents. The Gospel begins with only a title (1:1) and without any story of Jesus' birth. A brief introduction (1:2-13) quickly narrates John the Baptist's preaching and Jesus' baptism and temptation. The section 1:14-15 announces the occasion for the beginning of Jesus' ministry (the arrest of John the Baptist) and a summary of his preaching. Jesus' ministry in Galilee (1:16—5:43) is told with emphasis on his many healings and his conflict with the religious leaders. The section climaxes with the story of the raising of the little girl thought to be dead (5:35-43).

In the second part of the Gospel (6:1—9:50), Jesus' ministry within and outside of Galilee continues, as does also the accent on his gracious, miraculous acts, including the feeding of the multitudes (6:30-44 and 8:1-10). The section culminates with Peter's confession of Jesus as the Christ, the first of Jesus' three predictions of his death and resurrection, and his transfiguration (8:27—9:13). Jesus' journey to Jerusalem is briefly recounted (10:1-52).

The final section of the Gospel (11:1—16:20) focuses on his ministry in Jerusalem, beginning with his entry into the Holy City, a number of teachings (including those regarding the last days in chapter 13), the celebration of the Passover with the disciples, his arrest, trial, crucifixion, and resurrection.

Distinctive Features. The uniqueness of this Gospel lies in its emphasis on both Jesus' suffering and that of his followers. The Gospel poses a tension between the manifestations of Jesus' identity and the way that identity remained concealed until the crucifixion (see 9:9). Jesus commanded his disciples not to tell others who he was. His disciples consistently failed to understand Jesus and finally left him to die alone. Even his female followers refused to share the news of his resurrection. Even though the Gospel makes clear that Jesus is the Son of God (1:11), the only human in the narrative to acknowledge that fact was the soldier at the foot of the cross (15:39). This fact epitomizes the evangelist's view that the identity of Jesus is ironically revealed only in his suffering and death. Finally the Gospel is unique in that it may have originally contained no accounts of the appearances of the resurrected Christ, even though later scribes appear to have attached such accounts to the document (16:9-20).

Date and Purpose. The composition of Mark is associated with the Jewish revolt against Roman oppression, A.D. 66-70, and is usually dated just prior to or soon after 70. It was motivated in part by the persecution—or at least by the impending possibility of the persecution—of Christians. The Gospel was written, therefore, with emphasis on the suffering of Christ in order to prepare Christians for oppression.

LUKE

Authorship. This Gospel gives us no insight into the identity of the writer. Tradition has tried to fill that gap by identifying the author with Luke, the physician, a traveling companion of the apostle Paul (see Colossians 4:14). The theory gains support from a series of passages in the Acts of the Apostles in which the first-person pronoun, "we," is used (see Acts 16:10-16). Since it is commonly believed that the same author was responsible for both the Gospel of Luke and the Acts of the Apostles, the use of "we" may indicate the author traveled with Paul. But contemporary scholarship often holds that there is insufficient evidence to sustain this identification, and the identity of the author of the Gospel of Luke remains unknown.

Contents. Luke has five major divisions after a prologue that states the author's purpose (1:1-4). The first part is comprised of the narratives of John the Baptist's and Jesus' wondrous conceptions and births (1:5—2:52). The narrative of Jesus' birth in Bethlehem is a masterpiece of literature that has been highly valued throughout Christian history. The story from the boyhood of Jesus (the visit with his parents to the temple in Jerusalem) in 2:41-52 is unique in the Gospels.

The second section, 3:1—9:50, describes the beginnings of Jesus' ministry. The preaching of John the Baptist, Jesus' baptism, his genealogy, and his temptations are found in 3:1—4:13. His Galilean ministry occupies our attention in 4:14—9:50. Jesus announced his mission in Nazareth (he was rejected, however), healed people, taught, and called disciples. Among Jesus' teachings in this unit is a series of sayings uttered in the presence of a crowd on a "level place" (6:17-49), some of which are parallel to those found in Matthew's sermon on the mount. After several healings and the feeding of the five thousand, the climax of the section comes with Peter's confession of Jesus as the Christ, two of Jesus' three predictions of his death and resurrection, and his transfiguration (9:18-36).

The third part is a long narration of Jesus' journey to Jerusalem (9:51—19:27), dominated by his teachings, including a number of parables (among them the lost sheep, lost coin, and lost son in 15:1-32). But also included here are the accounts of the mission of the seventy disciples and their return (10:1-24), Mary and Martha (10:38-42), the cleansing of the ten lepers (17:11-19), and the story of Zacchaeus (19:1-10).

The fourth section is devoted to Jesus' ministry in Jerusalem (19:28—22:46), including the entry into the city and his teachings there. The last supper with his disciples and his prayer on the Mount of Olives are followed in 22:47—24:53 by the story of Jesus' arrest, trial, death, resurrection (including his appearance to two disciples during their walk to Emmaus, 24:13-35), and ascension.

Distinctive Features. Probably the Gospel of Luke is best known for its reporting of a number of beloved and remarkable parables, most especially that of the good Samaritan (10:29-37). This simple story is a response to the question, "Who is my neighbor?" (verse 29) and presents a model for Christian behavior. It concludes with the direct command, "Go and do likewise." But the story surprises us by depicting one of the despised Samaritans as the hero. It is he who acts out of love for one in need (the neighbor), while those of whom we might expect exemplary behavior "pass by on the other side."

The parable of the good Samaritan suggests several of the distinctive features of this Gospel. First, one of those features is the attention given to the parables of Jesus, many of which are preserved for us only in Luke. Second, the parable exemplifies the way in which the Gospel of Luke focuses on the outcasts of Jesus' day, for instance, Samaritans, tax collectors, lepers, and even women. In doing so, the evangelist stresses the universal appeal of Jesus' ministry. Connected with this theme is the Gospel's teaching regarding the plight of the poor and the dangers of wealth (for example, 16:19-31). In addition to the features represented in the parable of the good Samaritan, this Gospel takes care to relate Jesus to the historical setting of the time and to insist that a divine plan is being worked out in Jesus' ministry. More than any of the other Gospels it stresses the role of the Holy Spirit and prayer in Jesus' life. Jesus is portrayed as an innocent, forgiving man who unjustly suffers death. Also distinctive about Luke are the poetic hymns found in the early chapters (including 1:46-55 and 1:67-79), several of which have become standard parts of the church's liturgical tradition.

Date and Purpose. The probable date of the writing of Luke is between A.D. 75 and 85. The purpose of the writing is expressed in 1:1-4. It claims to offer a more accurate account of Jesus in order that the truth may be known. But Luke is a historical narrative told with the purpose of influencing the readers' moral and religious convictions, most especially to demonstrate that Jesus' ministry universally addressed all persons and that his death was unjust.

John

Authorship. By the end of the first century of the Christian era the author of John was associated with Jesus' disciple, John. Popular imagination further specified the unnamed disciple "whom Jesus loved" mentioned in the Gospel (see 13:23) as John, son of Zebedee, and the author of the fourth Gospel. However, the Gospel itself never divulges the identity of the author to its readers, leading to numerous conjectures that include Lazarus, Mary Magdalene, and John the Elder (see 2 John 1 and 3 John 1).

Contents. The story of Jesus in John is divisible into four parts. John starts by telling of two beginnings to Jesus' ministry (1:1-51). The prologue (1:1-18) sets the Gospel narrative in a context beyond space and time ("In the beginning," 1:1). The second beginning entails the historical inauguration of Jesus' ministry (1:19-51) and relates John the Baptizer's witness to Jesus, as well as the gathering of the disciples.

The second major part (2:1—12:50) tells of how Jesus revealed God's presence through impressive works and speeches. It begins with the first "sign" of Jesus' identity, the changing of water into wine at a wedding, and the cleansing of the temple. The section is dotted with Jesus' discourses, such as the one with Nicodemus (3:1-21). The feeding of the multitude and the long discourse that follows it (chap. 6) functions as a turning point in the narrative of the second part. Hostility and opposition to Jesus mounts between chapters 6 and 11, moved along by Jesus' ministry in Jerusalem and culminating in the plot to have Jesus executed.

The third division (13:1—20:29) has two main subsections. In chapters 13–17 Jesus privately prepares his disciples for his impending death with a series of long discourses and a prayer. Chapters 18–20 recount Jesus' arrest, trial, crucifixion, and three resurrection appearances.

The final part of the Gospel concludes the Jesus story with two segments: 20:30-31 and chapter 21. The latter passage reports another appearance of the risen Christ and his conversation with Peter.

Distinctive Features. John is unique among the Gospels. This Gospel powerfully presents Jesus as the Son of God and his claim on people's lives. It stresses Jesus as the revealer of God and the necessity of belief in Jesus. Jesus is the divine Son who partakes of a special relationship with God, his Father, and is even called God (1:1 and 20:28). He descends to earth to make God known and then returns to his heavenly home with his Father. His teachings have to do only with his identity as one sent from God, and his marvelous acts are presented as signs of his identity. The Gospel of John is known and loved for its many "I am" passages, with Jesus declaring, "I am the bread of life" (6:35), "the light of the world" (8:12), "the good shepherd" (10:11), and "the resurrection and the life" (11:25). The death of Jesus is presented as Jesus' enthronement as king. The Jesus of this Gospel claims that eternal life is a possession of the Christian in his or her present life and promises the sending of the Holy Spirit, the Counselor, after his departure. John sets the story of Jesus in the context of Judaism and three trips from Galilee to Jerusalem for the celebration of the Jewish feasts.

But perhaps the most famous passage, John 3:16, best summarizes the distinctive teaching of this Gospel. Out of divine love, the Son of God was sent into the broken and alienated world for the purpose of rescuing humanity from its own death and providing us with eternal life.

Date and Purpose. This document is most often thought to have been the last of the four Gospels to be written, between A.D. 90 and 100, but might well be dated as early as 75–85. Its purpose is explicitly to win the reader to faith in Christ (20:30-31), but implicitly to define Christian identity over against Judaism, possibly soon after the first readers had become separated from their religious home in the synagogue.

Historical Narrative

ACTS

Authorship. The author of this writing is believed to have been the same person responsible for the Gospel of Luke (compare

88

Luke 1:1-4 and Acts 1:1 and see the section on Luke above). Acts continues the story of the origins of Christianity begun in the Gospel of Luke, focusing on the early church and its missionaries, especially Paul. The author may have been a traveling companion of Paul's (see the "we" used, for instance, in 20:7-15), but that view is often challenged. While we can safely assume that its author was the same individual responsible for the Gospel of Luke, we cannot specify exactly who that person was.

Contents. Acts is divided into five main sections, as suggested by 1:8. After a prologue (1:1-5), an account of Jesus' final commands to his followers, and his ascension (1:6-11), the first section tells of the spread of Christianity throughout Jerusalem (1:15—8:3). The Holy Spirit is given during Pentecost (2:1-42) and provides the church with power for its community life, including its preaching and healing.

The second section concentrates on the outreach of the Christians into Samaria (8:4—10:48). In this section we are told of the call of Paul (9:1-19) and his preparation for ministry. Peter's vision (10:9-16) led to the conversion of the first Gentiles (those who have had no relationship with Judaism).

The third section (11:1—15:35) relates the extension of the message to Antioch and beyond. The early ministry of Paul and the apostolic meeting at which the mission to the Gentiles was formally sanctioned are recounted.

A fourth section (15:36—19:20) informs us of Paul's missionary travels through Asia Minor, Macedonia, and Greece. It contains accounts of, among other narratives, Paul's call into Macedonia by means of a vision, his speech in Athens, and his ministry activity in Philippi, Thessalonica, and Ephesus. The final section (19:21—28:31) concentrates on Paul's further journeys, his return to Jerusalem, arrest, and transportation to Rome. This segment features Paul's defense of himself before a crowd in Jerusalem, the Jewish council, and Roman officials. The story ends with Paul under house arrest in Rome.

Distinctive Features. Acts is unique in its attention to the spread of the Christian message and its story of the ministry of Paul. This book tells us how the church grew from a small, uncertain, underground group in Jerusalem (1:12-14) to a movement empowered by the Spirit of God that turned "the world upside down" (17:6). The well-known saying of the risen Christ at 1:8 summarizes the main thrust of the book. Christ promises the power of the Holy Spirit—a promise fulfilled in the very next chapter in the story of the Pentecost experience. With that power, Christ goes on to promise, "you will be my witnesses" in every known part of the world. The promise of the gift of divine power for faithful witness guides the ministry of the church throughout the narrative of Acts, even as it continues to guide the church today. The author of Acts shows how the church was obedient to the command of the risen Christ and became his witnesses to "the ends of the earth."

As the author tells the story, the reader is informed of the essential content and the universal appeal of the Christian message, as well as the power of the Holy Spirit to lead believers. Paul's missionary work is told in terms of three journeys: 13:4—14:28, 15:40—18:22, and 18:23—21:17. Paul is portrayed as a bold representative of the Christian movement who, while remarkably successful in his efforts, endures endless conflicts and persecution, crowned by his unjustified arrest in Jerusalem. Throughout its narrative Acts is notable for the adventure, suspense, and even the humor of the stories.

Date and Purpose. Acts was likely written A.D. 80–85 with several purposes in mind. It was intended to show how Christianity was congenial with Roman rule. But it was also concerned to present the early church as a model for Christians of the author's own time, most especially in terms of the church's inclusion of all people and its dependence on the guidance of the Spirit. That presentation of the early church was also intended to highlight the place and importance of the church's obedient witness to its

Lord. Acts also sought to present Paul's story and to commend the controversial apostle to its readers.

The Letters of Paul

The apostle Paul is the most influential of the authors of the New Testament in helping us understand how faith in Christ transforms daily life. The writings attributed to Paul represent the largest portion of the New Testament, thirteen of the twenty-seven books. They are most often dated within the years A.D. 49–58 of Paul's ministry that spanned the period of approximately 32–60. Those writings are letters addressed either to one congregation (for example, 1 Corinthians), or possibly a group of congregations (Galatians), but also include at least one written to an individual (Philemon). Like our own correspondence, these letters are responses to specific situations of which Paul had been informed. They constitute one side of conversations between Paul and those whom he addressed. Like much modern correspondence, the letters of Paul assume and build relationships between the sender and the receivers of the letters. In the process of writing, however, Paul expressed his fundamental Christian beliefs and the basic morality that arose from those beliefs. While his guidance is offered for very specific and concrete situations, it affords the readers insight into more general convictions held by the author, as well as his own deep faith.

Some scholars believe that not all the letters attributed to Paul are actually from his own hand. They propose that the circle of disciples gathered around Paul during his ministry continued to write under his name after the apostle's death. Such a practice was common in the ancient world. It represented an effort to keep Paul's teachings alive and relevant by relating them to new situations in the early church. There is, however, seldom doubt that Paul was the author of Romans, 1 and 2 Corinthians, Galatians, Philippians, Philemon, and 1 Thessalonians. About the others there is considerable debate. Among some authorities, but not all, the Pauline authorship of Colossians and 2 Thessalonians is doubted. Most often Ephesians, 1 and 2 Timothy, and Titus are thought to have been written by Paul's followers. In our New Testament all the letters attributed to Paul are generally arranged in the order of their decreasing length (the longest, Romans, coming first and the shortest, Philemon, occupying last place).

ROMANS

Authorship and Date. The letter to the Romans is thought to have been written about A.D. 56 from Corinth during Paul's last journey. It is the only known letter Paul wrote to a congregation he had neither established nor visited. Still, it is clear that he has some knowledge of the situation of the Christians living in Rome and speaks to that situation.

Contents. Romans is comprised of five major parts in addition to an introduction and conclusion. The introduction (1:1-17) includes the usual features of Paul's letters (author, addressee, greeting, and thanksgiving), but here Paul adds his claim to apostleship and a brief Christian creed. In the first major section (1:18—3:20) Paul sketches the universality of sin and the human need for a new relationship with God. The second section (3:21—4:25) describes what God has done in Christ to create the possibility of such a new relationship. That description centers on the act of God in Christ as the "righteousness of God" that restores the relationship of humans with their Creator. The appropriate human response to God's action is a trusting acceptance, which Paul calls faith.

The third section (5:1—8:39) explores the results of the new restored relationship, particularly in terms of the freedom it affords humans. Those pages speak of the Christian's baptism, the relationship of law and sin, and life in the Spirit. The fourth section (9:1—11:36) addresses the implications God's redeeming act has for the relationship between Jews and Gentiles and expresses confidence that the Jewish rejection of Christ will not terminate their relationship with God. The ethical implications of the divine act are discussed in the final section (12:1—15:13), including concerns for the authority of governmental leaders, relationships between the weak and strong, and Christian hospitality. The conclusion comes in 15:14-33 and asks for the support of the Roman Christians for Paul's intended missionary journey to Spain. Chapter 16 includes greetings to individuals in Rome known to Paul, an appeal to reject those who cause dissension, and a final benediction.

Distinctive Features. The uniqueness and importance of Romans lie in its careful articulation of the basic Christian belief, namely, God's justification of sinners through grace to be received in faith. For good reason, then, Romans 3:23-25 is one of the best-known passages from the letter. The universal human condition, that passage asserts, is sin and separation from God. But in Christ God has liberated humanity from the grasp of alienation from its Creator. The act is done purely out of grace—unmerited love—and can only be received by utterly trusting that grace. Among the other most-loved passages in Romans are 5:1 (another statement of justification by faith), 8:1-2 (there is no condemnation), 8:28 (all things work together for good), 8:31-39 (nothing can separate us from the love of God in Christ Jesus), and 12:1-2 (transformation by the renewal of our minds).

Romans gives us the clearest and most logically constructed evidence of Paul's beliefs. It is here we learn among other things of Paul's understanding of sin, grace, freedom, baptism, and the Christian community. Romans is also notable for its emphasis on the relationship between Jews and Christians and the agony Paul expresses as he discusses the issue of the destiny of his own people.

Purpose. The purpose of Romans is often debated, but most likely Paul was writing to prepare the readers for his visit with them and to win their sponsorship of his further mission in the west. It seems also to have been an effort to resolve the tension between Christians in Rome who had come out of a Gentile background and those who had come to Christianity from Judaism. Paul may have known of some friction between these groups in the Roman church and tried to resolve it with his theological insight concerning what holds all believers together, as well as his guidance on matters of Christian behavior.

1 CORINTHIANS

Authorship and Date. Paul wrote 1 Corinthians from Ephesus (16:8) in A.D. 54 or 55 during what most believe was his third missionary journey (Acts 18:23—21:17). It may have been the second of Paul's letters to this congregation, since 1 Corinthians 5:9 refers to an earlier correspondence with them.

Contents. First Corinthians addresses a series of issues pertinent to the congregation in Corinth. Paul first discusses the disunity and dissension in the church (1:10—4:21). He corrects both the tendency of the Corinthian Christians to align themselves in groups according to the apostle who introduced them to Christianity and the arrogance of some who claim to have a wisdom that surpasses that of other Christians. In contrast to these claims of wisdom, Paul speaks of the apparent foolishness of God in Christ. He proceeds to certain problems of immorality reported among the Corinthian Christians—an immorality that justifies itself on the basis of a pretense of a higher wisdom (5:1—6:20). He counsels Christians not to associate with those in the church who are guilty of immorality, that grievances be settled without recourse to lawsuits, and that sexual morality prevail among them. Then he turns his attention to questions raised in a letter he had received from the Corinthians (7:1—16:4). This long section includes his views on marriage (7:1-40), eating meat offered to idols and Christian freedom (8:1—11:1), relationships between women and men (11:2-16), disruptions in the common meal (11:17-34), spiritual gifts (12:1—14:40), and the resurrection of the dead (15:1-58). Directions for the collection for the Jerusalem church occupy Paul's attention in 16:1-4. He finishes the letter with discussions of his travel plans (16:5-9) and of Timothy and Apollos and their activities (16:10-12), followed by a conclusion (16:13-24).

Distinctive Features. The passage most commonly associated with 1 Corinthians is the celebrated hymn about love in chapter 13. There the apostle shows, first, that no gifting is ultimately of value unless it is accompanied and undergirded by compassionate care for others (vv. 1-3). Then he describes the kind of love about which he speaks (vv. 4-7). Finally, he returns to the relationship of love and other divine gifts, especially prophecy and knowledge, again to show that love is preeminent (vv. 8-13). The hymn stands on its own merit, but its power is even more evident when we acknowledge its context in the letter. Paul is trying to overcome the competitive and divisive spirit among the Corinthians, the boasting in their individual gifts. The "more excellent way" (12:31) is the way of love.

This letter provides readers a window through which to see Paul dealing with a young Christian congregation on issues such as that of competition among those with different gifts. It informs us how Paul related his understanding of Christianity to the problems that arise in living the faith. Most notable are his responses to the problems of divisions within the congregation, the arrogant claims of superior wisdom, and doubts about the resurrection of the dead. His effort to cultivate order in the church, while still honoring the freedom of life in the Spirit (chaps. 12–14), is of interest, too. But all of this is framed by Paul's conviction about the centrality of the cross and the resurrection. With the cross he begins his discussion (1:18-25) and with Christ's resurrection—and ours—he concludes it (15:1-58). All else is to be considered in the light of Christ's death and resurrection!

Purpose. The letter appears to have been Paul's response to news he received about matters in the church at Corinth. He refers to information he has learned through "Chloe's people" (1:11), and a letter from the congregation (7:1), as well perhaps as other sources of news (see 5:1). The purpose of this letter is to respond to these bits of information and in the process nurture a vital and unified community of faith in Corinth.

2 CORINTHIANS

Authorship and Date. This letter is thought by most scholars to be the combination of two separate letters Paul wrote to the Christians in Corinth. The earliest of these pieces of correspondence is found generally in 10:1—13:10, and the fragment of a later letter in 1:1—9:15. If this is so, the two letters were probably written around A.D. 55 or 56 from Ephesus and/or Macedonia during Paul's third missionary journey (Acts 18:23—21:17). Second Corinthians 6:14—7:1 may also preserve a portion of Paul's first letter to this church, written before 1 Corinthians and referred to in 1 Corinthians 5:9.

Contents. The contents of 2 Corinthians are made clearer when we understand that the document may be the blending of at least two different letters. As it stands, 2 Corinthians contains two distinct parts written in different tones. In chapters 1–9 Paul writes in a reconciliatory tone. He presents an autobiographical portrayal of himself in 1:8—2:17 in which he stresses his sincerity as an apostle and explains his visits to the Corinthians and others. The section in 3:1—6:10 comprises a defense of his ministry in which he contrasts himself with others (apparently other Christian missionaries who had influenced the Corinthians' view of Paul and his message). In 6:11—7:16 he issues an invitation to reconciliation. Within this section, 6:14—7:1 deals with the relationship of Christians and unbelievers and represents a sudden shift of tone and subject in the discussion. In 7:2-16 Paul expresses his joy that the Corinthians have accepted his earlier defense of himself and now have had a change of heart regarding him. Chapters 8 and 9 are devoted to his appeal for the collection on behalf of the Christians in Jerusalem. Second Corinthians 8:1-15 argues for generosity in supporting the cause, and 8:16-24 describes Paul's companions and their work in the effort. Chapter 9 expands his request for the readers' support.

In chapters 10–13 (the theoretical second of the letters comprising our 2 Corinthians) the tone is pained. Paul vigorously defends himself against vicious charges leveled against him by certain persons, perhaps other missionaries, in Corinth. He argues for his authority as a genuine apostle in chapter 10, responding to charges that he is a coward, weak, and given to boasting. In 11:1—12:13 he contends his boasting is justifiable, coming as it does out of his sense of weakness and suffering. His impending visit with the Corinthians is the subject of 12:14—13:10. Second Corinthians 13:11-12 concludes the letter; 13:13 may have been added when the two letters were joined together. (The Revised Standard Version separates verse 12 into two verses with the result that the benediction is verse 14 and not verse 13 as it is in the New Revised Standard Version.)

Distinctive Features. Certainly the distinctiveness of 2 Corinthians is its autobiographical quality. Here we gain insight into Paul's understanding of himself and his ministry. Throughout the letter Paul is his own advocate, and it is interesting how he goes about this task. He defends himself on the basis of God's grace, not his own merit. The frail nature of the servant of Christ (4:7-18) and the ministry of reconciliation that arises from God's reconciling act in Christ (5:16-21) are among the highlights of this letter. But so, too, is the solidarity of the Christian church demonstrated in Paul's appeal for the collection for the Jerusalem church (8:1—9:15). Here is the famed pronouncement, "God loves a cheerful giver" (9:7), and here, too, is the apostle's conviction that aiding the needy is an important expression of Christian faith.

Purpose. The purpose of the two component letters of 2 Corinthians is to reestablish a good relationship with the Corinthian Christians after that relationship had been damaged by misunderstanding and animosity. It pleads for understanding and reconciliation between the congregation and its human "parent," as well as assistance in the apostle's effort to aid the Jerusalem congregation in its crisis.

GALATIANS

Authorship and Date. There is considerable debate about the date of Galatians, but none about its Pauline authorship. The letter reflects a personal quality that most agree is characteristic of Paul. The problem of the date of the letter centers on the question of whether the churches to which Paul wrote were in northern or southern Galatia. If they were in northern Galatia, then the letter was likely written from Corinth or Antioch during Paul's second missionary journey (Acts 15:40—18:22) around A.D. 51–52. If they were in the southern part of the province, then the letter possibly came from Ephesus or Corinth during its author's third journey (Acts 18:23—21:17) around 53–54.

Contents. After a brief address and salutation (in which a thanksgiving for the readers is conspicuously absent compared to, for example, Philippians 1:3-5), Paul expresses his astonishment at what has happened in the Galatian churches since his visit there (1:6-9). He then launches into a defense of his apostleship (1:10—2:21). In his defense he makes the central point of the letter: Christians are brought into a right relationship with God through grace alone and no obedience to Jewish law is required (2:15-16). The argument soon shifts to an exposition of his understanding of the Christian gospel (3:1—4:31). The subject in chapters 3 and 4 pivots around the weighty topics of law and gospel, law and faith, and law and grace. In 5:1—6:10 he discusses the responsible use of Christian freedom, insisting on that freedom while maintaining that Christian liberty entails moral behavior. He writes a final warning to the readers in his own hand (rather than dictating it to a secretary) and concludes with a brief benediction (6:11-18).

Distinctive Features. The irate tone of the letter is its most distinctive quality (see 1:8 and 3:1), as is the way that anger is expressed in broken and wandering sentences (2:1-10). But the incensed tone only evidences the importance of the central topic of righteousness by grace not law. In terms of its content the unique feature of the letter is its defense of grace and freedom over against efforts to compromise these foundational blocks of Christian faith. The letter is the supreme statement of the danger of Christians betraying the essential gospel message by assuming that one must win God's love through righteous acts.

Among its best-known passages is 3:28 in which Paul affirms the unity of Christian believers in Christ. In that community, baptism into Christ diminishes to nothing the social differences that so often divide humans. The differences of ethnic origin, societal status, and gender all disappear into the oneness Christians know in Christ.

Purpose. The letter was written to correct the Galatian tendency to abandon the gospel Paul had preached in favor of another understanding of Christianity. It appears that, after having accepted Paul's proclamation of the gospel (grace through faith), the Christians of the Galatian churches had been lured into believing that circumcision and obedience to the law of Moses were required of them. In the process Paul's reputation had been tainted by his opponents who were advocates of circumcision. (Circumcision in the Judaism of the time was the act by which one took upon himself the obligation to fulfill the whole law.) Paul attempts, therefore, to set the readers straight about his own apostleship and the gospel he preached.

EPHESIANS

Authorship and Date. There is considerable doubt that Paul was the author of this letter, at least in its present form. Many scholars are persuaded that this letter is instead the work of one of Paul's followers because the vocabulary, style, and doctrinal teaching of Ephesians differ from Paul's genuine letters (Romans, for example). One-third of Colossians appears in Ephesians, suggesting that the author copied portions of Colossians. If this letter was written by one of Paul's disciples, it is to be dated toward the end of the first century of the Christian era. On the other hand, those who argue for Paul's authorship place it among the "imprisonment epistles," Philippians and Philemon (and possibly Colossians), and date it either A.D. 54–55, while the apostle was in prison in Ephesus, or 56–58, while he was confined in Rome. Whether written by Paul or one of his disciples, Ephesians may have originally been a letter intended for general circulation, with "in Ephesus" filled in at 1:1 for its use in that particular congregation.

Contents. After an introduction that is longer than many of those found in Paul's letters (1:1-23), the letter has two main parts. The first part is a statement of the salvation effected by God's act in Christ and the second the implications of that salvation for Christian living. In the letter's first component the author discusses a typically Pauline subject: the results of God's grace for Gentiles (2:1—3:21). As a result of the author's ministry, the Gentile readers have been brought from death to life by God's mercy and are given peace with God.

The second major part explores the implications of the grace-filled life, beginning with a plea that the readers lead lives expressing their new status with God, in contrast to those who have not accepted the gift of grace (4:1—5:2). The section 5:3—6:20 contains instructions on a variety of subjects, including sexuality, speech, and life within the Christian household. The section concludes with a metaphor that compares battle armor to the resources a Christian has for life (6:10-20). A commendation of Tychicus and a benediction complete the letter (6:21-24).

Distinctive Features. Ephesians is notable for its emphasis on God's purpose achieved in Christ (1:4, 9) and on how that divine plan entails the unification of all reality in Christ (for example, 4:4) who is the "head" of that new reality. That new unity is expressed in preliminary form in the church. The church is the body of Christ and Christ is its Lord, goal, and source of power for growth. No other New Testament book stresses as forcefully as does Ephesians the way in which God's grace creates a new, unified humanity. A well-known passage from Ephesians, 2:13-16, exemplifies these features. There Christ's work is pictured as peacemaking, demolishing the wall of hostility that had divided humanity into two great camps: Jewish people and Gentiles. With that wall down, there is a new creation—a single humanity formed around Christ.

Purpose. Ephesians was written in an effort to achieve a stronger sense of the oneness of the church at a time when Gentile Christianity was flourishing but was equally threatened with division over matters of belief and the lingering temptation to lapse into pre-Christian morality. Armed with the message of God's act in Christ, the author attempted to combat both the divisiveness and the immorality that endangers the church. The book teaches how humans can find an experience of unity in Christ.

PHILIPPIANS

Authorship and Date. That Paul wrote this letter is seldom doubted. It is clear, too, that he was in prison at the time of the writing (1:7, 13, 17). But the place of that imprisonment is uncertain, since we have indications that Paul may have been imprisoned on several occasions. The uncertainty of which prison held Paul when he wrote this letter makes dating the writing tentative. However, the letter most likely was written during Paul's imprisonment in either Ephesus or Rome. If it was written from Rome, the date of Philippians is likely A.D. 56–58. If he was held behind bars in Ephesus when he wrote this letter, it should be dated 54–55.

Contents. After the usual introduction and an unusually joyful prayer of thanksgiving for the readers and their faith (1:1-11), the body of the letter begins with Paul's reflections on his imprisonment and the possibility of his imminent death (1:12-26). In 1:27—2:18 Paul urges the readers not to be misled by certain of their opponents. The key to steadfastness, he suggests, is found in imitating the humility of Christ. In his confinement Paul tells the readers of his plans to send Timothy and Epaphroditus to them and writes commendations for each (2:19-30). At 3:1 the discussion turns to the subject of perseverance against dangerous temptations, most especially lapsing into either a dependence on obedience to the law of Moses, on the one hand, or a moral license, on the other hand (3:1—4:1). Philippians 4:2-9 presents a series of appeals: for reconciliation between two persons in the congregation, for confidence and peace, and for concentration on the worthy things. Paul thanks the readers for their gifts (4:10-20) and closes with greetings and a benediction (4:21-23).

Distinctive Features. The letter is dominated by a powerful, poetic description of Christ's sacrifice (2:6-11) that may have been an early Christian hymn quoted by Paul. This often-read passage fortifies Paul's appeal for humility by depicting Christ's humble actions. He surrendered his heavenly status, emptying himself, to accept the status of an obedient servant—a posture that led finally to his death on the cross. But because of his humble submission, God exalted him to the supreme station as Lord. Paul derived his understanding of the Christian life-style from the model we have in Christ.

While the letter addresses serious dangers confronting the readers, it is marked by both contemplative and joyous moods. In this letter we find Paul struggling with his destiny as he ponders the possibility of his execution. He longs to be united with Christ in his death. But, for the sake of others, he knows it is best that he continue his ministry in this world (1:23-26). Because of the somewhat disjointed contents of the letter, it is sometimes argued that the present document is the result of a joining of fragments of two or three separate letters written by Paul to the Philippians.

Purpose. The letter has several objectives. The first is to share with the readers the author's own personal struggles. The second is to warn them against the dangers of their opponents but to assure them that in Christ they have the strength to withstand those who would lead them astray. The third is to express gratitude to a congregation that had been supportive of Paul and his work.

COLOSSIANS

Authorship and Date. In some circles it is proposed that this letter came from the hand of one of Paul's disciples rather than from the apostle himself. The proposal is based on the fact that the style and vocabulary of Colossians differs from those found in the unquestioned letters of Paul (such as Romans and Galatians). If it is the work of a follower of Paul's, it is probably to be dated soon after his death, perhaps A.D. 60–64. Those who maintain Paul was the author usually group it with the other letters Paul wrote from prison—Philippians and Philemon—and date it accordingly—54–55, if the imprisonment was in Ephesus, and 56–58, if it was in Rome (see Colossians 4:3). It is sometimes thought that Colossians contains a portion of an authentic letter of Paul expanded by a later Christian author.

Contents. Following his greeting, Paul gives thanks for the faith of the Colossian Christians and assures them of his prayers for them (1:1-14). In 1:15-23 he announces the universal preeminence of Christ and the reconciliation Christ has accomplished. He then describes his own ministry to the church in the context of God's eternal purpose (1:24—2:7). At 2:8 the subject and tone shift to warning. The readers are in danger of succumbing to false teachings and thereby enslaving themselves to "elemental spirits of the universe" (2:8—3:4). The final part of the body of the letter is comprised of appeals that the readers live in a way consistent with the preeminence of Christ (3:5—4:6). Those appeals include one for love and peace, as well as a description of the desirable relationships among the members of the

103

Christian household. Final greetings and a signature in Paul's own hand end the letter (4:7-18).

Distinctive Features. The leading themes of this letter are three. The first is the divine plan of salvation expressed in the term *mystery* (1:26) and how the Christian has insight into and has experienced God's mysterious intent. Christ reveals God's grand design for the redemption of humanity. The second theme is the universal status of Christ, and its majestic expression is found in the poetic words of 1:15-20. The third theme is expressed in 3:1-4. Because Christians already have been raised with Christ to a new existence, our lives are in him. Hence, our highest goals are in Christ, not in this world.

Purpose. The Christians of Colossae were threatened by misleading teachers who propagated views Paul regarded dangerous to the church. Their teachings are characterized as "philosophy and empty deceit" (2:8), perhaps a conglomerate of religious and philosophical beliefs. The author attempts to combat the influence of this peril by focusing the readers' attention on the status and function of Christ, who is superior over all the forces of the universe.

1 THESSALONIANS

Authorship and Date. This book has the possible distinction of being the earliest of Paul's letters known to us. The authenticity of Paul's authorship is seldom doubted. It is widely believed that it was written about A.D. 51 from Corinth in the midst of the apostle's second missionary journey (Acts 15:40—18:22).

Contents. After the salutation (1:1), Paul expresses his appreciation for the Christians at Thessalonica (1:2-10) before beginning an explanation of his ministry among them (2:1-16). In 2:17—3:13 he recounts how he sent Timothy to continue his work with the readers. Instructions for the Thessalonian Christians are contained in 4:1—5:22. Those directions incorporate the ethical demands of the Christian life (4:1-12), including sexual purity.

Some among the readers are guilty of idleness, and the author urges them to become active. In 4:13-18, he reassures the readers that Christians who have died will be raised and united with Christ at his reappearing. That topic leads Paul on to a discussion of the "day of the Lord" in 5:1-11, climaxing in a plea for faithfulness. First Thessalonians 5:12-22 is a collection of miscellaneous instructions, including another appeal to those who are idle. Paul's conclusion comes in 5:23-28.

Distinctive Features. The notes of thanksgiving for the readers and their faith are dispersed throughout the letter (1:2-10; 2:13; 3:9-10), setting other topics in a positive context. Likewise, appeals are made in settings of encouragement (see 5:9-10). Beyond the skillful way Paul attempts to nurture the readers, this letter is notable for its description of the reappearing of Christ— its suddenness, the catastrophic events preceding it, the descent of Christ, and the resurrection of the dead. In this regard the letter is the earliest preserved written expression of these Christian themes.

Purpose. A report from Timothy, whom Paul had sent back to Thessalonica, spurred the apostle to write this letter (3:6). Timothy apparently reported to Paul some of the issues in the congregation, in particular, the charges that Paul was engaged in missionary activity for his own profit, the fact that some of the Thessalonians were passively awaiting the coming of Christ, and the confusion about the destiny of Christians who had died before Christ's reappearing. Paul's purpose in the letter is to address those issues and nudge the readers on in their Christian maturity.

2 THESSALONIANS

Authorship and Date. There is some dispute as to whether this letter reflects the thought of Paul himself or one of his disciples after Paul's death. Most often the letter is attributed to the apostle and held to have been written from Corinth about A.D. 51–52 while Paul was on his second missionary journey (Acts 15:40—

18:22) and soon after he had received a response to 1 Thessalonians. However, some think there are reasons to attribute it to a later Christian figure, perhaps between A.D. 70 and 90. These scholars contend that the problems addressed in the letter are more typical of the church later in the first century (for example, the view that Christ has already reappeared).

Contents. The introduction to the letter begins its main theme with an announcement of the righteous judgment of God (1:1-12), and then the discussion concentrates on the "day of the Lord" and the events that will signal its approach (2:1-12). That decisive day has not yet come, the author asserts, because certain events must first occur. Not the least of those events is the advent of "rebellion," "the man of lawlessness," and the "son of perdition." The fearful character of the events of this time is diminished, however, by the author's reassuring thankfulness that the readers are safe within God's love (2:13-17). A series of appeals is the final part of the body of the letter—appeals for prayers, activity rather than idleness, and obedience (3:1-15). A benediction, a signature in Paul's own hand, and a blessing are the last words of the letter (3:16-18).

Distinctive Features. What distinguishes this letter is its attention to the last days before Christ's reappearance and the language in which the events of those days are described. That language is "apocalyptic" in that it conceives of the final events as an upsurge of evil forces and pictures those evil forces as persons (for example, "the man of lawlessness"). Aside from the book of Revelation, 2 Thessalonians is the New Testament document that is most vivid in its description of these final events. The letter suggests the kind of confusion that may arise among those who have only recently become Christians and exemplifies a gentle pastoral guidance.

Purpose. The readers have been deceived into thinking that Christ's reappearance has already occurred (2:3), and the author attempts to correct their misconception. The correction is attempted by stressing the occurrences destined to precede Christ's reappearance and insisting that the readers had not yet experienced those events. The purpose of the letter is above all to reassure the readers, while at the same time instructing them to mature their views.

The Pastoral Letters

Authorship and Date. The letters of 1 and 2 Timothy and Titus are all attributed to Paul and addressed to persons known from Acts and/or elsewhere to have been coworkers with Paul. For instance, Timothy is mentioned in Acts 16:1-3 and 1 Thessalonians 3:2, and Titus in 2 Corinthians 8:16-24. Because they give instructions to those engaged in the leadership of the ministry of congregations, these letters are called "pastoral epistles." They are also grouped together because they share a common vocabulary and style, as well as purpose. However, their traditional association with Paul is frequently challenged, and instead they are credited to one of Paul's later disciples. The arguments against Paul's authorship of these three are numerous. It is claimed that their language and literary style, as well as their theological teachings, are distinctively unlike Paul. Information about Paul in these three is not always consistent with what we know of him from Acts and his letters (for example, the reference in Titus 1:5 to Paul's leaving Titus in Crete). The false doctrines attacked in the pastoral letters and the ecclesiastical officials ("elders," "bishops," and "deacons") discussed there are thought to be more typical of the church later in the first century than of Paul's time. If the view is that Paul was not the author of these three, they are most often dated about A.D. 100 or even later. Those who maintain that Paul is responsible for the writing of the pastoral letters frequently argue that their uniqueness among the apostle's correspondence is due to two facts: They were written late in his life (perhaps after 60) and were addressed to individuals with whom Paul had a long-standing personal working relationship, making them quite different from the apostle's letters to congregations. A compromise position holds that these three writings contain fragments of the genuine letters of Paul, revised and expanded by a later editor and author.

Purpose. The two letters to Timothy and the letter to Titus share a common purpose. They instruct the readers on how they are to behave in their leadership roles in the church. Specifically, these writings urge pastors to preserve the teachings of the church by rejecting false doctrine, maintaining order and good worship, nurturing godly lives through good example, and selecting leaders who are responsible and irreproachable.

1 TIMOTHY

Contents. The contents of 1 Timothy alternate between alarms sounded against misleading teachings and guidance for the churches under the care of the reader. The author begins with a typical Pauline introduction (1:1-2) and immediately moves to a central topic: warnings against false teachings (1:3-20). The false teachings focus on speculative matters. Such teachings corrupt morals as well as confuse minds. The author appeals to Paul's personal experience as a basis for warding off these misleading views. Instructions for the leadership of the church—guidelines for prayer and the selection of bishops and deacons—occupy 2:1—3:16. The topic returns to false teachings in chapter 4, this time with attention to how the reader is to interpret and nurture parishioners in the author's views. First Timothy 5:1—6:2 turns back to guidance for the congregations with particular attention to the treatment of certain groups of people: widows, elders, and slaves. A final plea for the reader to teach these things and be a moral, faithful servant of God finishes the letter (6:3-21).

Distinctive Features. Characteristic of 1 Timothy is the seriousness with which deviant teachings in the church are taken and the importance of practical, pastoral guidance of the congregation. Here we find the clearest delineation among bishops, deacons, and elders. But equally important is the view of Christ expressed in 2:5-6 and 3:16.

2 TIMOTHY

Contents. A salutation and thanksgiving (1:1-5) introduce a description of the faithful church leader, modeled after Paul's own life (1:6—2:13). That leader is to be courageous and loyal like a good soldier. More admonitions for the quality of the leader are explored in 2:14—3:9. Timothy is to be diligent in his concentration on the Christian virtues, such as gentleness and control of speech. Interspersed among these appeals for sound leadership are cautions against immoral and deceiving persons who threaten the church. A final charge and some instructions for the reader conclude the main part of the letter (3:10—4:18). The charge is to preach and live the truth in the midst of tendencies to ignore and distort it. The instructions include several dealing with the details of a personal visit with the author. Greetings to and from others and a benediction comprise the final verses (4:19-22).

Distinctive Features. The experience of Paul is used as a model for instructing Timothy, and personal testimony is woven into the argument at nearly every turn. The ideal character of the church leader is described in abundant detail. The church is presented as the preserver of true doctrine. That role is even more crucial because the church itself is infected with those who would lead it astray.

TITUS

Contents. The introduction (1:1-4) is followed immediately by a description of qualified elders and bishops in contrast to unworthy and deceptive persons (1:5-16). The remainder of the letter is occupied with admonishments to nurture proper belief and behavior in the church (2:1—3:11). Titus is urged to teach morality to all ages and all classes. He is to remind them of the character their lives should have as Christians even as they live in an environment that is not conducive to such character. Titus himself is urged to avoid theological controversies that blur his central focus. Practical instructions are given for dealing with one who is divisive in the congregation. Scattered among these pleas to teach proper doctrine and morality are statements of the transformation effected by God's merciful salvation (2:11 and 3:4-7). A few personal instructions, greetings, and "Grace be with all of you" complete the letter (3:12-15).

Distinctive Features. Confused belief leads to immoral behavior. This is one of the clearest teachings of Titus. But clear, too, is the idea that belief and morality arise from the good news of what God does in human lives: the Christian moral imperative is rooted in the redeeming act of God in Christ. Elders and bishops are described as the two classes of official leaders of the church.

PHILEMON

Authorship and Date. Philemon is the one letter attributed to Paul and written to an individual about which there is no doubt that the apostle was truly the author. Though not technically a pastoral letter, it is included in that category here for simplicity's sake. Like Philippians, it is a letter written from prison (v. 10), and therefore like Philippians (and possibly Colossians) is dated either during Paul's imprisonment in Ephesus (about A.D. 54–56) or in Rome (about 56–60).

Contents. After the salutation (vv. 1-3), the letter begins with a thanksgiving (vv. 4-7) that subtly makes Philemon receptive to Paul's request. Paul asks Philemon to accept back his runaway slave, Onesimus, as a Christian brother and not as a slave (vv. 8-22). Paul confesses he would like to keep Onesimus with him but thinks it better for the once-slave to return to his former master. Paul uses his influence on the reader, rather than invoking his authority to command Philemon to obey (vv. 8-9). The letter ends with greetings and a blessing (vv. 23-25).

Distinctive Features. This short letter is distinguished by the skillful, gentle persuasive powers of its author. Those persuasive techniques are of several kinds. Paul reminds Philemon that he is indebted to Paul (v. 19). He alludes to his God-given authority (v. 8). He addresses the letter to the whole congregation, so that Philemon becomes answerable to the entire community (v. 2). Finally, Paul suggests that he will later visit Philemon to see how he acted in this situation (v. 22).

This letter exemplifies how Paul understood that relationships among Christians transformed the established social relationships of the day. While Onesimus is to return to his master, the relationship between the two is different because they are brothers in Christ.

Purpose. Onesimus has run off from his master, Philemon, an affluent convert to Christianity as a result of Paul's ministry. The slave then meets Paul, and also becomes a Christian. Paul apparently convinces Onesimus to return to Philemon and writes this letter to prepare for his return. The goal of the letter is to convince Philemon to accept Onesimus as a Christian brother and not impose upon him the death penalty—the usual punishment inflicted on runaway slaves. Some speculate another motive in Paul's writing: to convince Philemon to free Onesimus of any obligation in order that the former slave might remain with and serve Paul (vv. 12-14).

Hebrews and the "Catholic Letters"

Beyond the four Gospels, the Acts of the Apostles, the letters attributed to Paul, and the Revelation of John, there are eight additional documents that comprise the New Testament. Several characteristics set these eight writings apart from their companions. The first is that (with the two exceptions of 2 and 3 John) they do not seem to be letters in the strict sense. Although some appear to have certain of the features of letters in their day (for example, James 1:1), they each prove to be something other than formal correspondence. In contrast to this shared feature, 2 and 3 John are most clearly letters and are among the best examples of first-century correspondence in the New Testament. The second common characteristic of these writings is that they seem to have been intended for general circulation among Christian churches. Again, 3 John is an exception to this, for it is addressed to an individual in a single congregation. But generally, as opposed to the majority of the letters of Paul, they were not addressed to specific congregations but were written for a wider readership.

The church early began speaking of seven of these documents (excluding Hebrews) as the "catholic epistles" (*catholic* means "universal"). But that label is less than adequate, not only because the writings are not all letters but also because in many cases they are not universal in their intended readership. Therefore, it is best to regard this segment of the New Testament as a miscellany of writings in various forms. We group Hebrews with the catholic epistles only because it fits no other grouping. Only because 2 and 3 John are associated with 1 John are they included among the catholic epistles.

HEBREWS

Authorship.   An author is never identified in this document. This fact has led to wide-ranging speculation that has resulted in identifying the author with Paul, Apollos, and Luke among many others. A case can and has been made that its author was a female Christian leader. The belief that Paul wrote Hebrews (see 13:23) was popular for a time, but can no longer be sustained. The author's identity still remains a mystery. Nonetheless, of that person we can say that he or she was of Jewish background (although highly influenced by Hellenistic and Gentile Christian thought), was well schooled, and possessed ability to argue points carefully and subtly.

Contents. The central place of Christ in Hebrews is indicated immediately in the introduction (1:1-4) where the author declares that Christ bore the stamp of God's nature, sustained the universe, and redeemed humanity. Christ's superiority to all other beings is asserted at the very outset. Thus the author begins a writing that has two fundamental parts. The first is an argument for the superiority of Christ and the meaning of this for Christians (1:5—10:39). The second is a proclamation of the witness to faith found in the Old Testament (11:1—13:19).

That Christ is superior to all the angels is the focus of 1:5—2:18. He stands above the angels, because he is God's own Son. But because he became human, was tempted, and suffered, he is the Christians' high priest. As the chief high priest, Christ is superior to all other priests (3:1—10:39). He is like, yet superior to, Moses. Christ is able to keep Christians faithful, whereas Moses was not able to prevent Israel's unfaithfulness (3:1—4:13). In the line of the first priest, Melchizedek, Christ qualifies as God's true priest (4:14—7:22). Because of the sinful humanity of all other priests, they must make atonement for their own sins, whereas Christ is human and at the same time perfect. Therefore, the old priesthood was inadequate to bring humanity to God. But as the chief high priest, Christ inaugurates a new covenant between God and humanity (7:23—10:39). Living eternally, Christ is able to save all who come to God through him. His priesthood takes place in heaven and is not confined to earth as was the old priesthood. Even though Jesus' sacrifice was done only once, it is effective for all time, for Christ ascended to heaven where he continues to serve as the mediator for all persons in all times.

Thus the author completes the first part of the writing and then goes on to argue that Christians are sustained in their faith by previous witnesses. The Old Testament witness to faith and its implications for Christian life occupy 11:1—12:29. Those witnesses believed that for which they hoped. Because Jesus suffered, Christians understand suffering as the disciplining of the children of God. On the basis of the sure foundation of witness to the faith

113

the author makes a final appeal for Christian living (13:1-19). That appeal embraces a wide range of topics such as hospitality, contentment, respect for leaders, endurance in suffering, and prayer. The book closes with a final benediction and the greetings (13:20-25).

Distinctive Features. "Now faith is the assurance of things hoped for, the conviction of things not seen" (11:1). This famous description of faith anchors the argument of the second part of Hebrews and introduces one of its unique features. The certainty of the content of hope and the commitment to what is beyond the physical senses is characteristic of the lives of the great figures of the Old Testament (11:4-40). It is this "cloud of witnesses" (12:1) surrounding the readers that enables them to sustain their faith through difficult times. There is hardly a more compelling affirmation of the strength found in the faithful witness of others than in this feature of Hebrews.

Another of the most distinguishing characteristics of Hebrews is its literary type. It is not a letter but something more closely resembling an ancient sermon based on the exposition of Old Testament passages (see, for example, Psalm 8:4-9 in Hebrews 2:5-9). Its manner of argument is also distinctive. The author systematically alternates between the announcement of a belief and an admonition for the reader to act in a certain way (1:1—3:6 and 3:7—4:13). But also unique about Hebrews is its view of Christ. The author understands Christ in the light of Old Testament concepts and stresses his humanity and suffering. It is through his suffering that the power of sin is broken and Christ achieves his perfection. He is both the high priest who offers the sacrifice and the sacrifice itself. Therein lies the final distinguishing mark of Hebrews: Suffering is a means of Christian maturity.

Date and Purpose. Hebrews may be dated about A.D. 95. Its title was not in the earliest copies but was added to later copies of the document because the author consistently stresses that Christians share the Jewish heritage of the Old Testament. (See, for instance, "our ancestors" in 1:1 and "the descendants of

Abraham" in 2:16.) It was written in a situation in which Christians were experiencing persecution for their faith and had little hope that the crisis would become anything but worse. Many were falling away from the faith (2:1; 3:14), and amid their difficulties the readers had lost their enthusiasm for Christian living. Hebrews was written to instill confidence and nurture endurance. It gave the readers' suffering new meaning by its appeal to Christ's suffering and admonished perseverance on the basis of the power of the witnesses to faith surrounding Christians.

JAMES

Authorship. The author identifies himself as James (1:1), and tradition has equated this James with the brother of Jesus (see Mark 6:3 and Acts 15:13). However, that equation is no longer widely held for numerous reasons. Nonetheless, this James seems to have shared a background in Christian thought deeply influenced by Judaism, even though he wrote in a sophisticated Greek style. A more precise identification of the author remains obscured in the shadows of history.

Contents. James is comprised of a loosely joined series of moral teachings. In the first part the author states that trials and temptations come to all, and every worthy gift is from God (1:2-18). The injunction to act on what one is taught rather than be a passive hearer engaged in self-deception constitutes the next step in the author's argument (1:19-27). Impartiality in one's relationships is urged in 2:1-13, particularly as it has to do with the relationship between the rich and poor. The author maintains the necessity of acts of kindness (2:14-26). A faith that is not expressed in moral behavior is not a living faith. One way a living faith is expressed in behavior is through speech (3:1-12), for speech is a powerful tool. James 3:13-18 warns against prideful wisdom and claims that true wisdom is from God. A series of pleas for humility and resistance to the world is found in 4:1-17. In 5:1-6 the rich are warned how vulnerable they are to sin.

Assurance is given that the Lord will come, and patience and prayer are urged (5:7-18). James concludes with instructions for dealing with Christians who err in their ways (5:19-20).

Distinctive Features. "Faith by itself, if it has no works, is dead" (2:17). The most unique feature of this writing is the insistence that faith must demonstrate itself in moral action or else it is lifeless. James is especially important because of its insistence on the just treatment of the poor and the dangers of wealth. In form it is like a tract or perhaps a collection of pieces from sermons.

Date and Purpose. Most would date this writing late in the first century, perhaps around A.D. 90. It gives us no specific information about those to whom it was addressed. "The twelve tribes in the dispersion" (1:1) is a general allusion and could apply to nearly any Christian congregation. But the author seems to have understood the congregations in mind to be suffering from pride, the ill-treatment of the poor, and the delusion that as long as they gave lip service to the proper creed nothing else was demanded of them. James attacks such behavior and attitudes and seeks to correct them through this writing.

1 PETER

Authorship. The author claims to be Peter, the apostle (1:1) and an eyewitness to the sufferings of Jesus (5:1). Some interpreters take this as convincing evidence that the author was indeed the Simon Peter of the Gospels. However, for various reasons others doubt that the Galilean Peter was the real author. The matter remains unsettled in contemporary scholarship.

Contents. The letter contains two main parts: What might have been a homily from an occasion of baptism is found in 1:3—4:11 and instructions to Christians suffering persecution in 4:12—5:11. After an introduction that emphasizes the church is "chosen and destined" by God (1:1-2), the author discusses the hope Christians have as a result of their birth into the family of God

(1:3-12). This is followed by a description of the moral lives of those who are now "God's own people" (1:13—3:12), and a discussion of proper relationships with civil authorities and within Christian households. Attention is turned to suffering in 3:13—4:11. The author asks readers to be firm and courageous and to understand that by suffering they are freed from sin. Beginning at 4:12, the author acknowledges a "fiery ordeal" the readers are suffering; however, suffering is an occasion for joy, since it is shared with Christ. In 5:1-11 instructions are given for how to live in difficult circumstances. The letter ends with a greeting and benediction (5:12-14).

Distinctive Features. First Peter 2:9-10 summarizes one of the most important features of the writing. It offers a profound understanding of the church as a holy people ("a chosen race, a royal priesthood, a holy nation, God's own people") born anew by God's grace and commanded to live as God's priests in the world. It assures its readers that suffering is related to holiness and is to be understood in the light of Christ's suffering; to suffer means to share Christ's pain as well as his glory. Hence, it equips the reader for the experience of suffering by the context in which it places affliction and by the assurance it offers. The document may be the result of the joining of portions of two different sermons into what was circulated as a tract among congregations in a particular region.

Date and Purpose. If Peter, the Galilean disciple, was the author, the writing might be dated in the A.D. 60s during the persecution of the Christians in Rome at the hands of Caesar Nero. If another person wrote under Peter's name, the date is more likely around 95–100 when it was Caesar Domitian who oppressed the Christian church. In either case, the congregations for which this writing was intended knew the experience of persecution, and the author sought to fortify the readers for that experience.

2 PETER

Authorship. Whereas the author of this letter claims to be the same Simon Peter we know from the Gospels (1:1, 16), the majority of scholars think such an identification is more to honor Peter than to name the author. Passages such as 3:15-16 suggest a figure in the later church. Nor is it certain that this author is the same person responsible for 1 Peter. If its author was not Peter, she or he remains anonymous to us.

Contents. Because of what God has given Christians, they are endowed with hope and righteous living (1:3-21). But false teachers and prophets threaten Christian faithfulness (2:1-22). The author describes the erroneous views of these persons and their judgment before God. In 3:1-13, the writer turns to the reappearance of Christ and offers an explanation for why that long expected event has not occurred. A final warning against false leaders is followed by a doxology (3:17-18).

Distinctive Features. Many know the declaration of 3:8 ("with the Lord one day is like a thousand years and a thousand years are like one day"); it is one of the unique features of the book. The delay in the reappearing of Christ is due not to God's tardiness but to the divine measurement of time and God's desire that none should fail to receive mercy. Furthermore, the strong language used in 2 Peter's polemic against false leaders sets this document apart, as does its emphasis on the role of Scripture in the church. It is notable, too, that the author of 2 Peter seems to have used the letter of Jude (compare 2:1-18 and Jude 4-16).

Date and Purpose. Second Peter is often dated as the last of the New Testament documents to be written, between A.D. 100 and 150, because the issues addressed in the writing are those most often associated with the church at the turn of the century. The document intends to warn against deviant teachings in the church and to arm the readers against such misdirection.

1 JOHN

Authorship. First John never identifies its author by name. Tradition associated this letter with the author of the Gospel of John because of the similarities between the language of the two books, a view still advocated by some today. Others believe that the author was a leader of a number of congregations that knew and used the Gospel of John as its primary source for understanding Christian life and faith. This suggestion accounts for the similarities between 1 John and the Gospel of John, while not claiming that 1 John's author was the fourth evangelist.

Contents. An understanding of the argument of 1 John is difficult, since it often moves unexpectedly from one subject to another and repeats many points. It begins with a declaration of the basis of the church ("life") and the fellowship and joy of those who share that experience (1:1-4). Darkness and light are used respectively to speak of human sin and the hope God has brought into the world (1:5—2:11). Believers are victorious over the darkness of the world, and the world will pass away while believers continue ("abide") in their relationship with God (2:12-17). "Antichrists" perpetuate a lie, but Christians may be confident of their destinies when Christ reappears (2:18-29). In their love and the assurance that comes from their keeping God's commandments, the children of God are distinct from the children of the devil (3:1-24). The spirit of truth is to be distinguished from the spirit of error, typical of the antichrist (4:1-6). God's love evokes Christian love, and the experience of love among the children of God builds reassurance (4:7—5:5). Christ has appeared in human form, and there are three witnesses to the truth of his revelation, the most important of which is God's own witness in the divine Son (5:6-12). The confidence of faith is based on a knowledge that gives rise to moral behavior (5:13-21).

Distinctive Features. No other New Testament document so emphasizes the love of God and the way that love forms the foundation for Christian life. Indeed, the best-known verses from

1 John are doubtless 4:7-12, beginning, "Beloved, let us love one another, because love is from God. . . ." That central theme is one example of how 1 John shares the language and thought of the Gospel of John. Unlike the Gospel of John, however, it attacks, for example, those who deny Christ's humanity and those who fail to practice Christian love. It does so while reassuring the readers of the correctness of their life and faith. This document may be the collection of bits of sermons preached during a crisis in one congregation and then circulated among all of the churches whose lives were influenced by that crisis.

Date and Purpose. First John was written after the Gospel of John, perhaps A.D. 90–100. It was intended to reassure a community of faith in the midst of a crisis caused by the separation of some of its members. The document attempts, first, to describe the error of those who had chosen to dissociate themselves from the main body of the church and, second, to justify the views of the parent church.

2 JOHN

Authorship. The author is described only as "the elder" (v. 1). The association of 2 John with 1 John occasioned the identification of the author as John, and some features of this letter are similar to both 1 John and the Gospel of John. Still, we know the author only to be a leader among a group of congregations.

Contents. This letter begins with a salutation and a greeting (vv. 1-3). The two parts of the body of the letter are, first, a prompting to love one another (vv. 4-6) and, second, three warnings and an instruction (vv. 7-11). The readers are told to beware of deceivers, examine themselves, and guard the doctrine of Christ. They are instructed not to welcome into their midst anyone who does not hold the true view of Christ. The closing is an apology for substituting a letter for a visit and gives greetings from the author's church (vv. 12-13).

Distinctive Features. The central importance of the view of Christ and the love that exists within the church are the two most important contributions of 2 John. The drastic measure of denying hospitality to those who hold variant views of Christ suggests the importance of how one perceives Christ.

Date and Purpose. With 1 and 3 John this document should be dated after the Gospel of John, perhaps around A.D. 90–100. Its purpose was to alert congregations to the dangers posed by certain traveling representatives of a group that held an erroneous understanding of Christ and did not practice Christian love.

3 JOHN

Authorship. Like 2 John "the elder" (v. 1) is the author's only self-designation, but this letter became linked with 1 and 2 John and its author identified with the one responsible for the Gospel of John. There are, however, few similarities between 3 John and the Gospel of John. Most likely the one responsible for this letter is the same person who wrote 2 John, and we can say only that the author was a leader among a cluster of congregations.

Contents. The letter begins by saluting Gaius, its recipient (v. 1), with a prayer and a joyful thanksgiving for his life of faith (vv. 2-4). The body of the letter is comprised of two instructions and a commendation. The first instruction urges the support and extension of hospitality to other Christians (vv. 5-10). The second charges the readers to imitate what is good, not evil (v. 11). The behavior of Diotrephes is condemned, since he rejects the authority of the writer and refuses hospitality to others (vv. 9-10). Demetrius is commended (v. 12) and the letter concludes with an expression of the author's desire to visit Gaius, a blessing of peace, and greetings (vv. 13-15).

Distinctive Features. By means of 3 John we are allowed a rare peek into the internal relationships among certain early Christian churches. The letter is distinguished by its evidence of the limited role of persons of authority in these churches and by the use of persuasion to enhance authority.

Date and Purpose. Along with 1 and 2 John, this letter is dated after the Gospel of John, perhaps around A.D. 90-100. Third John reflects another occasion in the situation surrounding 2 John. Some representatives of deviant groups have been denied hospitality with the result that those from sister churches are not always warmly welcomed. Third John tries to encourage reception of traveling missionaries at a time when some of Gaius's congregation were overly suspicious of all such persons.

JUDE

Authorship. The author identifies himself as "the brother of James" (v. 1), but we have no idea to which James the reference is intended. "Jude" is a Greek translation of the Hebrew name Judas. However, it is unlikely that the author was Judas, brother of Jesus (see Mark 6:3), or Judas, the son of James and one of Jesus' disciples (see Luke 6:16, John 14:22, and Acts 1:13). The identity of this "brother of James" remains unknown.

Contents. This letter is a violent attack upon those who menace the church with fallacious teachings. The author describes such persons and observes how they have found their way into the church (vv. 3-4) before assuring the readers of the divine punishment awaiting such false teachers (vv. 5-16). Jude reminds the readers of how such disruption in the church was predicted during the "last time" and admonishes them to remain strong in the face of such threats (vv. 17-23). A benediction is found in verses 24-25.

Distinctive Features. Jude is unique in its passionate attack on those who would lead the church astray. It is distinctive, too, in its use of Jewish writings from the period after the completion of the Old Testament to support the author's views (see vv. 9-10 and 14-15).

Date and Purpose. Most date Jude early in the second century, perhaps as late as A.D. 140. Jude presumably undertakes to guard the church against the rising danger of the heresy called "gnosticism." It was a movement to deny the full humanity of Jesus and held that all material reality is evil.

Apocalyptic

REVELATION

Authorship. We know the author of this document only as "John of Patmos" (1:9) and as one who claimed to be a prophet in the Old Testament tradition (1:3). Efforts to identify this John with the authors of either the Gospel or the letters of John have been made, but it appears wiser to keep John of Patmos distinct and deal with his document on its own.

Contents. The intricate relationships among the various visions that comprise Revelation evade normal logic. Still, there is evidence of a careful artistic structure to the three major components of the book: the letters to the seven churches (1:4—3:22), the persecution of the Christian readers and its consequences (4:1—19:4), and God's victory over the forces of evil responsible for the persecution (19:5—22:5).

Revelation begins with a title and a blessing for those who hear and attend to the message (1:1-3). Revelation 1:4—3:22 presents the letters of John of Patmos dictated by the Spirit to the seven churches in Asia. After the formal address and John's commission (1:4-19), the letters to Ephesus (2:1-7), Smyrna (2:8-11), Pergamum (2:12-17), Thyatira (2:18-29), Sardis (3:1-6), Philadelphia (3:7-13), and Laodicea (3:14-22) are presented. Nearly every letter contains some description of the qualities of Christ (see, for example, 2:8), a commendation of the church for its good attributes (2:19), a condemnation of it for its faults (2:4), and some promise to those who "conquer" (that is, those who are faithful to God, 2:11).

The visions in 4:1—19:4 have to do with the divine insight into the meaning of the persecution and its consequence. The section opens in heaven with the Creator and the heavenly council and includes several hymns to the "Lamb" (4:1—5:14). The consequences of evil are vividly related in five interrelated scenes (6:1—19:4). The first describes the seven seals (6:1—8:5), each of which shows the results of evil in the world and/or the place of Christians amid its disastrous effects. The second scene depicts the plagues and woes of the seven trumpets (8:6—11:19). Each in this series of seven is interrupted by an interlude that pictures Christian martyrs (7:1-17 and 10:1—11:14). The third scene (12:1—14:20) constitutes an extended interlude in the depiction of the fruits of evil. Here the heavenly war between the forces of evil and God is recounted. The third series of seven, the seven bowls, is presented in the fourth scene (15:1—16:21). The bowls seem to represent natural and political plagues.

The persecution and its consequences conclude with a fifth and final scene, the portrayal of the fall of Babylon (Rome) in 17:1—19:4. The evil of Babylon is symbolized in the figures of the whore and the monster, the laments of heaven and earth, and the judgment of this evil empire. The final major part of Revelation pictures God's decisive victory over evil (19:5—22:5). The faithful are rewarded, evil is destroyed, and the millennium (a period of a thousand years) is established. Then comes God's ultimate triumph (20:11-15) and the new creation (21:1—22:5). The book ends with the invitation to heed its prophecy (22:6-21).

Distinctive Features.   Perhaps what is best known from Revelation is not a particular passage but a picture of a lamb. That is appropriate, for John's apocalypse is by nature pictorial. Also, the lamb is the dominant image of the Christ figure in this book. Christ who gave himself as a sacrifice is, through the sacrifice of his followers, now the triumphant lamb.

Revelation is distinctive in that it is the one full-length "apocalyptic" writing in the New Testament. That is, it reports a vision of what God intends to do in the future at the last days and does so through the use of elaborate images and symbols. Revelation is further distinguished by the way it encourages hope among Christians in a period of utter hopelessness, nurturing confidence that God's justice would ultimately triumph. Unique, too, is its view of suffering as a key instrument God uses to complete the divine plan for creation. Finally, no other Christian document so forcefully claims that God has not abandoned world history but continues to pursue the redemption of creation.

Date and Purpose.   Revelation is most often dated in the years between A.D. 95–100. It was written, presumably, amid or in anticipation of the persecution by Caesar Domitian of the Christians in Asia Minor. Christians were being commanded to curse Christ and pledge their allegiance to the Roman Caesar as their lord and god. Faced with what seemed the inevitable defeat of the Christian movement at the hands of the mighty Roman empire, John wrote his revelation of what all this meant in the divine plan for the world. He tried to encourage and empower Christians to withstand the potent onslaught of oppression and persecution. He helped them see beyond their grievous present to the final victory of God over all that opposes justice and righteousness. The purpose of Revelation was not to predict events that were to take place in future generations, but to address its own age with a message of hope—a message that is relevant in every generation.

Aurelia drew close and snatched the stallion's reins from the horseman. "I don't know why not. You're traveling to the edge of the kingdom in hopes of seeing more like him."

"And you're not?"

"I intend to see people as well as horses."

He snorted. "Waste of time."

She craned her neck to look for Robert. He stood on top of a heaping wagon and gestured with dramatic hand movements. Whatever he had said thus far, the frantic movement of servants and supplies had ceased.

"Drew," she said, returning her attention to the man at her side. "Your name wouldn't be short for Andrew, would it?"

He flinched. "Now how did you find that out?"

"I heard an interesting story the other day that reminded me of you."

"About a great horseman, was it?"

"No, the storyteller implied that when you see a person with extraordinary height, that person is from the Outer Realms. Is it true? Are you from the Outer Realms?"

Drew winked. "Well, now, Your Highness, if you want to know about the Outer Realms, maybe you should make that your next expedition."

"What are you saying, Fielding?" Robert stood at Aurelia's feet. "Don't start her on another trip. We haven't gotten this one going yet." A hand stretched up. "My reins, Your Highness."

She glared at him.

"Aurelia," he corrected.

"Giving up so soon?" she said, handing over the reins. "I thought you were going to get us under way."

"I am," he replied. "We're leaving."

Her head whipped around. The servants stood in two neat rows beside the doorway. The six guards had mounted all six horses and faced ahead. Both supply wagons sat secured with drivers holding the reins. And up in the balcony, her father, her stepmother, and her sister waited to pose for the moment of departure. Ready.

"Underrated him again," Drew muttered.

Aurelia turned back to Robert. "What are we waiting for, then?"

He touched the tip of his fingers to his forehead and motioned toward her. "Why, for you to give the command, my lady."

She took a breath and announced in a strong, powerful voice, "Move out."

Boots dug in. Calls sounded. Horses swung into action. Wagon wheels squealed as they lurched into rotation, and good-byes and good wishes poured from windows and doorways. Reins and bridles and saddles jangled with movement as Bianca fell into step beside Horizon.

Aurelia swept her head around, taking in one last view of the palace. Then she focused on the landscape beyond the arch of the palace gate. She urged her horse into the lead and felt the chain around her ankle break free.